I0407976

EIR (ISSN 0273-6314) *is published weekly
(50 issues), by EIR News Service, Inc.,
P.O. Box 17390, Washington, D.C. 20041-0390.
(703) 297-8434*

European Headquarters: E.I.R. GmbH, Postfach
Bahnstrasse 9a, D-65205, Wiesbaden, Germany
Tel: 49-611-73650
Homepage: http://www.eir.de
e-mail: info@eir.de
Director: Georg Neudecker

Montreal, Canada: 514-461-1557
eir@eircanada.ca

Denmark: EIR - Danmark, Sankt Knuds Vej 11,
basement left, DK-1903 Frederiksberg, Denmark.
Tel.: +45 35 43 60 40, Fax: +45 35 43 87 57. e-mail:
eirdk@hotmail.com.

Mexico City: EIR, Sor Juana Inés de la Cruz 242-2
Col. Agricultura C.P. 11360
Delegación M. Hidalgo, México D.F.
Tel. (5525) 5318-2301
eirmexico@gmail.com

Mission Countdown 2017

EIR Contents

www.larouchepub.com Volume 44, Number 14, April 7, 2017

CNSA

Cover This Week

China's phase-three planning for a planned 2017 robotic lunar exploration mission, which is to return samples from the Moon to Earth.

I. The New Mission on Earth and in Space

Celebrating Krafft Ehricke's 100th Birthday as the World Turns Toward Space

by Kesha Rogers

April 3—The LaRouche movement celebrated the 100th birthday of German-American space pioneer Krafft Ehricke last week. During the week-long tribute to his life and work, we made available a number of his writings and videos, and our presentations gave insight into Ehricke's visionary ideas of mankind's unlimited potential for growth and development throughout the Universe. The celebration included a remarkable conference in Munich, Germany, under the joint sponsorship of the Fusion Energy Forum and the Schiller Institute, titled "Realizing Krafft Ehricke's Vision for the Future of Mankind." This issue of *EIR* prints some of the conference presentations, thereby continuing last week's theme in an issue dedicated to Ehricke and titled "What is Science?"

On March 25, during the week of celebration, President Trump gave a speech—one that most Americans missed—as one of his Saturday morning addresses, that should have dominated the media airwaves. This five-minute address followed his signing of the NASA Transition Authorization Act by just a few days. Apparently none of the major media reported on this very important speech. Instead, they were overwhelmingly focussed on increasingly attacking the President and creating more mass hysteria with fake news of Russian hacking and healthcare failure. Meanwhile, you were

EIRNS/Stuart Lewis

Krafft Ehricke speaking at an event in New York City, Nov. 28, 1981.

denied the opportunity to witness and be moved by this inspiring address, given by the President to "renew our national commitment to NASA's mission of exploration and discovery."

In his short speech, the President declares, "This week, in the company of astronauts, I was honored to sign the NASA Transition Authorization Act ... We renew our national commitment to NASA's mission of exploration and discovery. And we continue a tradition that is as old as mankind. We look to the heavens with wonder and curiosity."

This renewed commitment to exploration and discovery spoke to the very principles that the great visionary Ehricke championed for the greater part of his life, as he continued to develop his ideas and vision for the future of mankind in the universe.

The international conference in Munich included prominent speakers on perspectives and prospects for science, technology, and space exploration.

On that day, the planets must have surely have been aligned in a special way. On the day that President Trump gave his address—which was accompanied by beautiful images from the Hubble Space Telescope—Swiss astronaut Claude Nicollier, who flew on two Hubble repair missions, gave a speech to the conference in Munich, and displayed some of the same images taken by the Hubble that the U.S. President was showing across the ocean in his weekly address.

For Space Exploration, the American System

President Trump's March 25 address came shortly after speeches he gave around the country that week (with very little media attention), in which he elaborated on the principles of the American System of economics, with emphasis on the contributions of great American Presidents and American System statesmen, including President Abraham Lincoln, Henry Clay, Alexander Hamilton, and others. President Trump has become the first President in 100 years to invoke the American System. The arc of these developments both nationally and internationally is very important in understanding the shift toward a new paradigm, toward a renaissance for all mankind, which is rapidly emerging throughout the world right now.

Consider President Trump's addresses in the context of another major development, Secretary of State Rex Tillerson's trip to China, where he invoked the commitment by the United States to the "principles of non-conflict, non-confrontation, and win-win cooperation." Tillerson's trip has opened the door to important, positive relations with China, which can only be enhanced in the upcoming meeting of President Trump and China's President Xi Jinping.

In his March 21 speech to the National Republican Congressional Committee Dinner, speaking on the Principles of the American System, President Trump declared, "We renew and emphasize our allegiance to the policy of protection, as the bulwark of American industrial independence and the foundation of American development and prosperity."

The American System of political economy has been the commitment and focus of Lyndon LaRouche and his movement for decades. Krafft Ehricke's emphasis was to end the zero growth paradigm that has been killing human progress, renew the understanding that there are no limits to growth, and realize what he called mankind's "extraterrestrial imperative."

This is the same outlook that President Trump developed toward the close of his address on March 25, just one day after Krafft Ehricke's 100th birthday. Trump said, "NASA's greatest discoveries teach us many, many things. One lesson is the need to view old questions with fresh eyes. To have the courage to look for answers in places we have never looked before. To think in new ways because we have new information. Most of all, new discoveries remind us that, in America, anything is possible if we have the courage and wisdom to learn."

With this renewed commitment to a national mission of space exploration, and the return to the principles of the American System of economics, we can once and for all break with the destructive policies of the so-called Anglo-American "special relationship," which rejected economic progress and the uplifting of the world's peoples. It should never have been allowed to take over U.S. policy. The escalating attacks against the President are precisely a result of his defiance of those destructive Anglo-American policies—destructive of our nation and the world.

The developments of the past week—our international conference in Munich and President Trump's March 25 address—highlight the direction toward a new set of relations among nations already emerging throughout the world and in the United States. The key to the success of such a vision will be the acceptance, by the United States, of the offer of "win-win cooperation" with China, to enable U.S. participation in, and contribution to the great potentials of the Belt and Road Initiative for a better humankind.

Munich Conference Honors Space Pioneer Krafft Ehricke

by Rainer Apel

March 26—An audience of 130 gathered at the Sheraton Arabellapark Hotel in Munich on March 25, for a one-day conference organized by the Fusion Energy Forum and the Schiller Institute, on the occasion of the 100th birthday of the German-American space pioneer Krafft Ehricke. The theme of the event was "Krafft Ehricke's Vision for the Future of Mankind," placing his work for a new paradigm of human existence in the context of the present-day effort of the New Silk Road.

After welcoming remarks by Werner Zuse of the board of the Fusion Energy Forum, who particularly welcomed Lyndon LaRouche who was attending the conference, three artists (Diana Milewa, soprano; Roland Albrecht, baritone; and Elena Arnovskaya, pia-

nist) introduced the event with three pieces: Josef Haydn's "Nun scheint in vollem Glanze der Himmel," aria from *The Creation*; and two songs by Franz Schubert, *An die Musik* and *Frühlingssehnsucht*. The artists also performed after the first break.

The first speaker, Marsha Freeman, *EIR* science editor and biographer of Krafft Ehricke, spoke on his "extraterrestrial imperative" which presented a vision of a human civilization that would finally be liberated from wars and poverty and make use of man's creativity the potential of which is unlimited. Ehricke's commitment to space exploration as the venue for this new paradigm was sparked by Fritz Lang's 1929 movie *Frau im Mond* (The Woman on the Moon) which he

EIRNS/Christopher Lewis

Marsha Freeman, EIR Technology Editor, addressing participants at the Krafft Ehricke's Vision for the Future of Humanity Conference *in Munich, Germany, March 25, 2017.*

Soprano Diana Milewa (left) and Baritone Roland Albrecht (right), performing at the Krafft Ehricke conference in Munich, March 25, 2017.

EIRNS/Christopher Lewis

saw in 1929 at the age of 12. During the early 1930s Ehricke wrote short fiction pieces portraying how human civilization had changed in the course of space exploration and colonization, as seen from a date in the future. He was always guided by the question: where will we live in 50 years, in 100 years from now? Focussing human creativity on the realization of this vision would finally, in his view, unify all peoples and nations; mankind would finally become mature.

In addition to his work on the technical realization of space exploration, Ehricke also was a prolific author on the political and social aspects of this entire process over decades. He made a special effort at the end of the 1960s to further elaborate his concept of the "extraterrestrial imperative," giving interviews and speeches, as well as writing articles and books. He did so explicitly as a fight against the rise of the rock-drug counterculture and the movement against nuclear power and against science, whose aggressiveness reminded Ehricke of the Nazi shock troops he had experienced in Germany at the end of the Weimar Republic.

Ehricke, who died of cancer in 1984 at the age of 67, had become a household word in the United States. His role in shaping the American space programs had made his name familiar to everybody. His designs for "Selenopolis," a permanent human settlement on the Moon powered by fusion energy, with a maglev transportation system, and for "Astropolis," a permanent station in space as large as a city—the logical step forward deeper into the Solar system, were visions popular throughout the United States and beyond. Ehricke's personal contribution to the development of space technology and the design of space missions is uncontested. Reviving his work for the present younger generation is a must.

A personal message from Krista Ehricke, Krafft's eldest daughter, who could not attend the conference, was then read to the audience. She portrayed him as a scientist totally committed to the development of space science and technology, but also a caring father, who always challenged his daughter to understand concepts and develop new ideas. She and the Ehricke family grew up in the immediate environment of the first U.S. astronauts of the Mercury, Gemini, and Apollo missions.

The three musicians performed several pieces after the first coffee break: *Ave Maria* for soprano by Giulio Caccini; two duets for soprano and baritone by Felix Mendelssohn-Bartholdy, *Ich wollt meine Liebe ergösse sich*, and *Volkslied*; and "Casta diva," an aria for soprano from Vincenzo Bellini's opera *Norma*.

China's Space Program

The second speaker at the conference was Jacqueline Myrrhe, a renowned freelance space journalist in Germany who also publishes the *Go Taikonauts!* journal. She presented the development of the Chi-

Poster of the movie Frau im Mond (Woman in the Moon) premiered Oct. 15, 1929, in Berlin, Germany.

nese space program from its announced start in 1958, through the highly disruptive periods of the Maoist "Great Leap Forward" and "Cultural Revolution" periods which prohibited real progress in Chinese space science and technology.

Myrrhe pointed out that only in the 1970s, did China's space sector make progress with work on a geo-satellite in 1981, and on a space station starting in 1992. The space sector has always been viewed in China as a science driver, with a priority on national economic and social development, in the broader perspective of the roadmap for progress until the year 2050. The Chinese space program may have been slow, particularly in earlier stages, but it has picked up pace and shows the absolute determination of the Chinese to turn plans into reality within a set timeframe.

EIRNS/Christopher Lewis

Helga Zepp-LaRouche (standing, right) addressing Krafft Ehricke's Vision for the Future of Humanity *Conference in Munich, Germany, March 25, 2017.*

Others, particularly the United States, may have been there first, but China is arriving there step by step. The space station, the lunar missions (first unmanned, then manned), and the Chinese Mars program, feature a resolute and optimistic development of technological and scientific capacities, and the entire future program is open for cooperation with other nations, as is the design for the New Silk Road, Myrrhe explained.

The afternoon session of the conference, which began with a speech by Schiller Institute President Helga Zepp-LaRouche, was introduced with a Chinese love song, performed by Feride Gillesberg-Istogu (soprano) and Benjamin Lylloff (piano).

Zepp-LaRouche spoke about her personal memory of Ehricke, whom she first met in the early 1980s and with whome she engaged in intense dialogue until his early death in 1984. Ehricke was characterized by a strong optimism; he was firmly convinced of the necessary evolutionary step mankind had to make to develop from a terrestrially-confined species to a space species. His view was that this would be an epochal change, comparable to the one which occurred from the Middle Ages to modern civilization, triggered by the Renaissance period. The New Paradigm which China is introducing with the New Silk Road strategy, is congruent with what

Ehricke designed and what the LaRouche movement has campaigned for for more than four decades: a new and just world economic system which will develop conditions appropriate to promote human creativity.

The New Paradigm poses a challenge to the old paradigm: the oligarchical system of Western globalization, characterized by inhuman axioms and defended by advocates who do not want to see it replaced. In this strategic context, Helga explained the issue of "Donald Trump:" the new U.S. President, whose declared plans pose a threat to the elites of the old system, is in fact being attacked by an unprecedented campaign of lies, black propaganda, and hatred, which cammpaign serves to defend of the doomed old paradigm, the British System.

In his most recent public speeches, in Detroit, Tennessee, and Kentucky, President Trump has addressed the importance of reviving the American system as practiced by Abraham Lincoln, Henry Carey, and George Washington. He has announced that he will:

• Invest $1 trillion in domestic infrastructure,
• Stop the regime change wars abroad, and
• Establish mutual cooperation with the two other world powers, Russia and China.

President Trump's upcoming meeting with China's President will—if it works well—bring a positive breakthrough in the global strategic situation, which is why President Trump is being attacked by the same intelligence agencies that worked for the old system, for Obama, and for the British. The task ahead for the United States is comparable to the one that Friedrich List defined when he wrote almost 200 years ago about the American System as an alternative to the British System.

The Chinese New Silk Road strategy, first formulated in 2013, has recruited 4.4 billion people in more than 60 nations into a global development program, in the range of $21 trillion, of projects along six land routes and one maritime route reaching out beyond Eurasia into Africa. The infrastructure development initiated by China in Africa, is largely congruent with the Africa plan presented by Lyndon LaRouche 30 years ago. Europe, which ought to play a constructive role with development in its neighboring continent, remains absent. But, the New Paradigm keeps marching forward, Zepp-LaRouche said.

Chinese and Western Thought

The advance of mankind onto the Moon, she explained, was seen by Ehricke as a process opposite to that which has occurred on Earth. Here, man arrived very late in evolution, whereas on the Moon, man will be the beginning of evolution. Lunar civilization will develop characteristics different from those which have dominated man on Earth. Mutual cooperation for the good of all others will have to be the basis of human life under lunar conditions. Harmony has to be at the center of relations there, just as it has to be at the center of the New Silk Road development, as presented clearly by China's leading official, Yang Jiechi, during his recent visit to the United States. The notion of harmony, as developed by Confucius and also by Nicholas of Cusa—who portrayed peace and harmony as only possible on the basis of all microcosms working for the benefit of each other. Zepp-LaRouche added, education in universal history and the best contributions of all cultures, should guide mankind in the future.

The second speaker of the afternoon session, former Swiss astronaut Prof. Claude Nicollier, reviewed of his personal "Steps into Space" which included four service missions at the Hubble Space Telescope carried out from the Space Shuttle. Nicollier, today President of the Lausanne Swiss Space Center, said he fully agrees with Ehricke that space is the necessary next step in human evolution. This is a challenge, as much as it was when Kennedy, in his famous Houston speech of

EIRNS/Christopher Lewis

Dr. Carl-Otto Weiss, former president and professor at the German Meteorological Institute, spoke on human creativity at the Krafft Ehricke conference.

September 1962, said that the Americans want to go to the Moon, not because it was easy but because it was hard, because Americans were confident they would have the capability to overcome all difficulties and make it to the Moon by the end of the decade—which they did.

The lunar exploration program was unfortunately terminated with the Apollo 17 mission, but the ISS was built, as was the Hubble Telescope for deep space investigation. These are important steps into space, and new manned missions have to follow, which Nicollier said he is optimistic will indeed follow.

Before the last speech of the conference, a message from Thomas Stafford was read to the audience, endorsing the revival of the Ehricke heritage. Stafford is a veteran U.S. astronaut beginning with his work on the Gemini missions, through the entire Apollo Program, and the orbital stations Salyut and ISS. Two videos were then shown: one from a Silk Road-connected new science initiative for the youth of Yemen, and another from a Leipzig-based team of German youth who have developed a prototype of a Moon rover, which won a contest last year at an international presentation of rovers in Huntsville. A video showing President Trump's endorsement and signing of the NASA Transition Authorization Act of the United States just a few hours before, was shown as well.

The concluding speaker, Prof. Carl-Otto Weiss, former president and professor at the German Meteorological Institute (PTB), spoke on human creativity being the only resource of mankind that can and will secure a future. The attacks on science by the green movement and the climate hoaxsters, have, since the beginning of the propaganda drive of the Club of Rome, caused a loss of optimism among the people. This propaganda, which Weiss described as a method originating in the interests of the economic-financial oligarchy of the Western system, has to be challenged with facts showing that the past inventiveness of man, in the course of his evolution allows confidence that all problems can and will be solved—by science, creativity, and development.

Climate change is not man-made. There is no scientific evidence whatsoever backing this ideology. The nature of climate is determined by other factors that have to do with the fact that the Earth is not a closed system, but embedded in the Solar system, and in the Universe, both of which have profound effects on terrestrial conditions. Green propaganda causes fear, and intimidated populations are easy to manipulate.

Ecologism is a new religion, which has replaced the churches as traditional partners of the ruling elites. Weiss stressed that there is no such scarcity of resources as claimed by this new religion. There is an abundance of raw materials, enough to guarantee supplies to mankind for thousands and millions of years. Mankind made his first big step in evolution with the discovery of fire; his next big step was the development of nuclear power. This will be followed by an even larger resource, nuclear fusion, Weiss said.

He also explained that for him, a particular aspect of the green propaganda is that it is the heaviest in Germany, and Germany is a target for a special reason: Anglo-American geopoliticians have always wanted to destroy the scientific-technological potential of Germany, especially its potential to work with Russia, which has been perceived as a mortal challenge to the Western system.

The conference was concluded by the Schiller Institute Chorus, singing "Va Pensiero," the "Chorus of the Hebrew Slaves," from Giuseppe Verdi's opera *Nabucco.*

Greetings to the March 25 Krafft Ehricke Conference

Krista Ehricke Conference Greeting

Good morning. My name is Krista Ehricke. I was asked by my friend Marsha Freeman, to speak a little about my father as I and my sisters knew him. You all know him as a far thinking space enthusiast and scientist. We knew him as simply our dad. My friends these days say, "Oh, your dad was a rocket scientist" and then there is that "rocket scientist" chuckle and no one knows what he really was all about. What you all know are his academic accomplishments, his innovative ideas, and his tremendous understanding of the human spirit. There are so many things to tell, but from my perspective the everyday things are those that others don't realize. He was brilliant, but he was so much more as a man and father. He valued his family and we valued him.

One of the truths in our house was that when my dad was at home, he was working, and we had to be quiet. Not an easy thing with three girls, and in the sixties that meant two little ones and a teen. I was the teen or the tween. My dad had a study in the back of the house which was his sanctuary and not to be entered by his screaming, playing daughters. My mother always said our father had important things to calculate and write, and we could not scream at the top of our lungs or run through the house like banshees, or we would give him a headache, which, of course, was not good.

I finally figured out how to spend more time with him, through my love of books. Of course he had a lot of multi-subject books in his study, so I would say I wanted to look at them and pick one to read. What parent would say no to a child that wanted to read?? Since reading was a quiet endeavor I always got permission to go into the inner sanctum. There, I would lay on the floor, on my stomach, legs crossed at the ankles, and I would generally end up with "The Rise and Fall of the Roman Empire". It was the one I liked the most. I found it very satisfying to just lay on the floor in front of his desk and read. I knew he was there and felt I was together with him. And if, on the rare occasion I had a question, I could ask and he would answer me. I thought this was the perfect set up.

We had the old fashioned family dinners, and most of the time my dad would be home. Our discussions were pretty vivid. My parents would steer the conversation to the news, or politics, or whatever family things needed discussion. Of course school would come up, but after that it was often the abstract subjects, such as politics, morality or philosophy, or even mythology. He would set up situations and then ask me, what would I do, or what did I think of something. He never told me I was wrong, he always waited for me to figure it out. He would steer me with a provocative question and make me think.

I later figured out that this was his way to stimulate my curiosity, because every time when I couldn't answer his question I would rush to the encyclopedias and look up the subject. We had four encyclopedia sets at home, so I could do a lot of reading to find the answers I wanted. I didn't like not knowing something, so this would push me to research for an answer. One thing that I remember so distinctly was never being exactly told I was wrong. Rather my father would ask me why I thought the way I did. If I could show him my thought process was solid, he would give me big kudos for the thinking, then he would gently suggest I take another look, or investigate further and tell him what I thought after that.

I was in high school during the sixties and President Kennedy's space race. My sisters are eight and ten years younger than me so they were quite young, and I had the greatest exposure to that excitement. My dad was on TV a lot in San Diego, and so I got a sort of notoriety of my own in school. I got interviewed by the press, and I told them lofty things about my ambitions. Of course none of that ever happened, but at the time I had the confidence of youth.

At that time, my dad was involved with the origi-

Krafft Ehricke with satellite models, Oct. 10, 1957.

nal team of astronauts. I was privileged to meet some of them and became very fond of Scott carpenter and Alan Shepard. If you knew my dad, you knew he hated things like press conferences, or cocktail parties where people just talked fluff, in other words the political side of the space race. He thought his time was wasted there and better spent behind his slide rules. On one occasion he had a press conference and dinner to go to, which he was quite annoyed about. He decided I should go in his stead and represent him there. My escorts were Scott Carpenter and Alan Shepard. Of course I was elated! I was in high school and being escorted by astronauts! This was important, so my mom and I picked out a green taffeta dress for me to wear.

The astronauts came to the house to pick me up. They were very cordial and protective of me and never left my side at the event. After dinner there was coffee and dessert. I was trying so hard to fit into this august group, that I spilled my coffee all over the front of my dress. Taffeta gets darker when it gets wet, so here I was, the entire front of me covered in coffee. I was horrified, as you might imagine, with these dark wet stains in plain view. These two men flanked me, trying their best to cover the front of me and still walk and talk on the way out, with flash bulbs and the press leading the way. Flash forward 25 years or so and I found myself at a Hall of Fame induction dinner, sitting next to Alan

Shepard. He smiled and asked me how that dress was with the coffee on it! I about fell over, but apparently it was a fun memory for him too.

I was fortunate enough, due to my age, to accompany my dad on various trips. My mom always stayed with my sisters and I was more than willing to go! One time we went to Houston to the Johnson Space Center. There was no launch pending so we were able to see the control center where all the guys sat during launch, wringing their hands in high stress mode. We got a private tour of the accessible areas. Everyone knew my dad, and I was beaming to be with him!

Another time my dad had to speak to Congress regarding budgets and costs and we flew to D.C. together. I spent the day racing in and out of museums. We went to the air and space museum together the next day. I also had the good fortune to go to Orlando with him, to the Kennedy space center, where I got to witness the launch of Apollo 15. My dad said David Scott was a great guy and someone he respected. That made the launch even more interesting. I didn't get to meet him and of course we sat a mile away in the bleachers. But even at that distance, the ground shook more than any earthquake I had ever been in, and the sky lit up and filled with smoke. It is definitely something you never forget!

The next time I would be in D.C. was in 1984 to accept the AIAA's Goddard Astronautics Award for my father who was too ill to go. It was only a few months before his passing. I accepted the award in his honor and was able to pass on his gratitude and speak for him to the group. Once again I was filled with pride.

He was a very kind man which I think is an important quality. He had emotional intelligence. When it came to matters of the heart he was always available. If you were sad or had a heavy heart he was the one to go to.

We adored my dad, and my friends felt the same way. He danced with us at my home parties and would join in to make up special dances. He stayed just long enough and left just soon enough. My friends always asked if he were home, because he would answer their questions. He had the ability to simplify his answers so regular people understood, even my high school friends, and they always felt like they had gotten a pearl of wisdom that others hadn't. That was the magic of my dad: he could explain anything to anybody, and he would do it until you understood, even if it took most of the night for you to get it!

My dad had a genius' mind, which was actually a difficult cross to bear, at least to me. I could see his visionary mind working so far ahead, in places the rest of us didn't have a glimmer of, and I thought that must be a burden or a frustration at the least. I asked him once, very pointedly, how he managed to keep repeating everything, how he managed to constantly be told his calculations or advanced thoughts were impossible, until they were also proven by others. To have his designs be seen as silly, such as Skylab, which was dubbed "Ehricke's orbiting outhouse." His response has stayed with me forever. Paraphrasing, he said," Krista, don't worry about me, I am ok. You see I have a core, right here in my center that knows exactly who I am and knows if I am right or wrong. It is my core that no one can ever enter, no one can take away from me, and that's where I know the truth and where I can go and am protected. It has saved me many times and it will never be breached by anyone." He amplified this and told me to search for that refuge within myself. I think I have succeeded. This was the personal philosophy that got him through any difficulties and is something I have never forgotten.

Greeting from Gemini and Apollo Astronaut General Thomas P. Stafford

I'd like to extend my greetings to the participants of the Schiller Institute conference celebrating the life and work of Krafft Ehricke.

Though I couldn't be there in person, I think that this conference is very timely. As someone who has been part of the U.S. space program since its very early days, from Gemini through Apollo, from the Apollo-Soyuz mission to our participation in the International Space Station today, I can tell you that to achieve these great things, we must have clear goals, and a vision. The ideas of Krafft Ehricke for lunar development and mankind's settlement of space can be looked to today for those far-reaching goals and that vision—especially for a return to the Moon, something that the United States turned away from 7 years ago, though I believe we can reverse that today.

I wish your conference the very best success.

General Thomas P. Stafford
Gemini and Apollo Astronaut

An Electronic Message From the Yemeni Pioneers

Introduction: We thank the Schiller Institute for extending this invitation to the Pioneers' Office in the Advisory Office for Coordination with BRICS (AOCB).
Ali al-Ghaffari,. Chairman

Pioneer Ali Al-Ghaffari, Chairman of the Pioneers

Good morning! Today is the 8th of March, which is the International Women's Day. On this occasion, we send our best wishes to the New Silk Road Lady, Mrs. Helga Zepp-LaRouche, and to all women and men of the world, via commemorating Dr. Kraft Ehricke. This occasion represents for us an inspiring event for our actions today and tomorrow, especially as the visions of Dr. Ehricke have topped the global agenda one hundred years after his birth.

I would like to welcome you all to the Remote Sensing Center at the Yemeni Ministry of Communications in Sanàa.

Pioneer Azzhra'a Mohammed al-Nunu

First we would like to extend our sincere thanks to Mr. Hussein Askary, who has been encouraging the Pioneers to study one of the most important sciences in human history.

Based on the vision of the Pioneer heroes, the chairman of our organization "Friends of the BRICS " wrote a groundbreaking text on a vision for the reconstruction of Yemen, explaining the metrics of progress and victory of the BRICS nations. This text was sanctioned by the great novelist Al-Gharbi Amran, and was translated to Chinese by the Friends of the BRICS in Yemen.

It represents a comprehensive program of action for us today, and a message of peace that space and rocket technology should be utilized for creative reconstruction, and not for destruction as the Anglo-Saudi aggressors are doing.

Pioneer Abdullah Ridwan Jaghman

The Special Report "The New Silk Road Becomes the World Land-Bridge" represented the nucleus for our thinking about space.

We believe that our sustainable path towards space will only be achieved by securing our right to national credit, and through achieving our goals for sustainable development 2030.

Pioneer Retaj Abdul Salam Aldar

The Space Silk Road is the new language of peace.

Pioneer Fajer Fouad

Join us to live in accordance with the 5 metrics of progress of the BRICS.

Teacher Mohammad Al-Ansi

One of the messages we send to the BRICS nations is our effort to teach the Chinese language once a week at the Café Mazaji, and we preparing to join the celebration of the International Day of the Chinese Language on April 20.

Pioneer Abdullah Yones Alademy

We call ourselves the Pioneers, because we, the children of the founders of the AOCB, are dreaming of becoming space explorers.

The idea of the Pioneers emerged to launch the concept of the Space Silk Road. In the same way, the AOCB launched the notions of the maritime and land New Silk Road here.

Ruba Aref Muthanaa Alameree

Pioneers, because we took the lead in building our organization on the basis of the 5 Metrics of Progress of the BRICS nations, through which we will face the challenges of our childhood.

Pioneer Mohammed Maeen
A Resident of Maryland, U.S.A.

Not only earth, but the entire solar system is our home, and the only limitations that exist are the ones we impose on ourselves. Our freedom starts with creating our own credits and financial resources. A necessary step to enjoy our freedom is to establish our own national reconstruction bank on Hamiltonian principles.

Fouad al-Ghaffari

The Pioneers have created a development process for childhood in Yemen.

Discussing space is not a fantasy, but rather the most basic notion of the human right of thought.

And it is the fourth element of the Four Laws of the economist Lyndon LaRouche to reform the world order on the basis of building the individual human being and culture, and not on the idea of economics as financial matters!

MUNICH KRAFFT EHRICKE CONFERENCE

China's Space Program—Hare or Tortoise?

by Jacqueline Myrrhe and Dr. William Carey

March 25—In the recent past China has introduced economic and political initiatives which promote its rise as a global power. Embedded in this process is its national space program, allowing the 'Middle Kingdom' to follow a very smart concept for a step-wise build-up. The basic principle is to develop key systems —such as launch sites, launchers—or tracking, telemetry, and control (TT&C) systems—which can be used across the different fields of space exploration: from Earth observation to the manned space program, lunar exploration or other areas. It is maybe a little bit like a Lego system or the menu of a Chinese restaurant.

Hare or Tortoise—Dynamic or Slow?

The hare and the tortoise story is about the proud and idle hare who thought with his long legs he is the fastest animal in the universe and can win any race. Day-by-day he was joking about the tortoise, saying: "You with your short legs will never achieve anything."

One day, the tortoise had enough of this and challenged the hare: "Listen, hare, only because you have long legs, you do not need to be so arrogant. And anyway, how can you know for sure that I am not able to run fast? Let's have a competition!"

In similarity with this fable, China's space program is looked at as being a slowly moving tortoise... Why did this stereotype come into being?

China's space program has the reputation of being:

- **Small:** Yes, it has a relatively small budget. The annual ca. $1.8 billion China spends on space, corresponds to roughly a tenth of NASA's annual budget or 30-50% of the European Space Agency's (ESA's) budget.
- **Slow:** China has not conducted many missions—so far there have been only 6 manned missions with 11 taikonauts involved (two of them flew twice).
- **Technologically less advanced:** It is based on copied Soviet-Russian technology.
- **Not significant enough:** China is not a major space nation because it has not launched relevant science missions, which are the strength of NASA and ESA.
- **And anyway:** China is pursuing military goals, space dominance, space super-power ambitions.

FIGURE 1

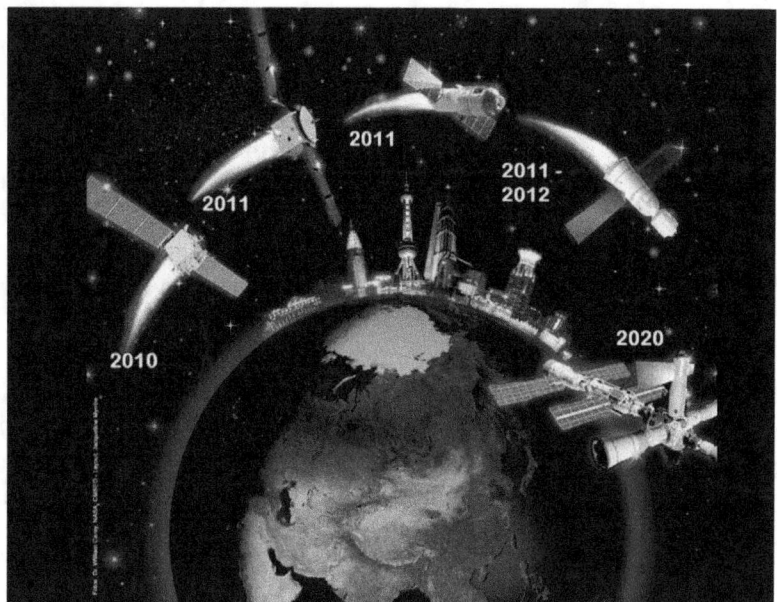

Relevant milestones in China's space program: From left: Chang'e 2; Yinghuo 1; Tiangong 1; Shenzhou; CSS.

Mission Countdown 2017   13

FIGURE 2
Milestones in China's Societal and Economic Development

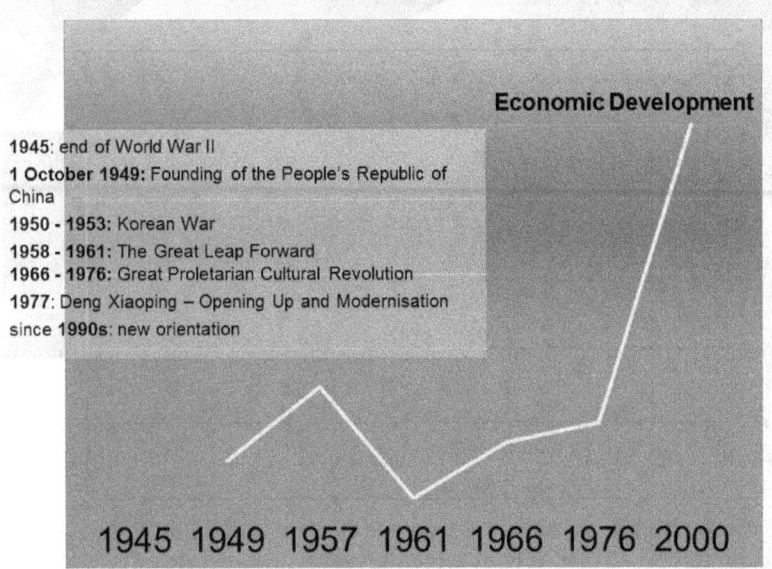

1945: end of World War II

1 October 1949: Founding of the People's Republic of China

1950 - 1953: Korean War

1958 - 1961: The Great Leap Forward

1966 - 1976: Great Proletarian Cultural Revolution

1977: Deng Xiaoping – Opening Up and Modernisation

since 1990s: new orientation

Economic Development

1945 1949 1957 1961 1966 1976 2000

So what is it then?

Is China's space program a dynamic hare or a slow tortoise?

Is it a threat to the world?

After a historical overview of the beginnings of the Chinese space program, the second part of the article will focus in on current developments.

Milestones in China's Societal Development

To understand China's space program it is necessary to take the societal and economic context into consideration. This is particularly important from the time after World War II until the turn of the millennium.

At a time when Western nations in Europe, the United States, and Japan enjoyed economic development and prosperity, the Chinese economy rode on a rollercoaster.

Until 1958 the Chinese economy experienced moderate growth. Initiated in 1958, the Great Leap Forward project was supposed to catapult China within 15 years into the league of leading industrial nations. After only 3 years however, the economy of the country was broken. The following Five Year Plan brought some relief, until in 1966 the Great Proletarian Cultural Revolution took its course. The persecution of intellectuals and academics damaged a whole generation of experts, teachers, the scientific elite—most of China's best talent. The economy during the Cultural Revolution did not completely stand still, but progress did. Only after the death of Mao Zedong could the situation halt. China's firsts in space are embedded into these dramatic decades of the nation's post-war development.

China's Firsts in Space: The East Is Red—DFH 1

As an outcome of the Korean War, China felt under nuclear threat and asked the Soviet Union for technical assistance in the development of its own nuclear capabilities including long-range missiles. The Chinese request was granted.

The launch of Sputnik 1 on October 4, 1957 by the Soviet Union sincerely impressed the "Great Helmsman," Mao Zedong. Such a satellite he wanted to have for his own nation, preferably with the support of the Soviet Union. China's space ambitions were not driven by a race. For China, the underlying principle was to catch up with leading technology developments in the world.

The Chinese Academy of Sciences (CAS) set up a task force for the technical and scientific development of an indigenous satellite connected to a long-term and comprehensive national satellite program. CAS was fully aware of the relevance of satellites for future national scientific and technical development. Chairman Mao advised his comrades:

> If we're going to throw one up there then throw a big one, one that weighs two tons. Of course we start throwing small, but with one that is at least two tons. Something like that chicken egg of the Americans, I won't do it!

Despite the Soviet Union supporting China's military missile program, there was no assistance in the civil space sector.

Worse, because of the Great Leap Forward, too few allocated resources and materials, and too small a work force made it impossible for CAS to succeed with a national satellite. Lack of progress and missing know-how made the Chinese experts realise that they had to start from scratch: developing sounding rockets first.

FIGURE 3

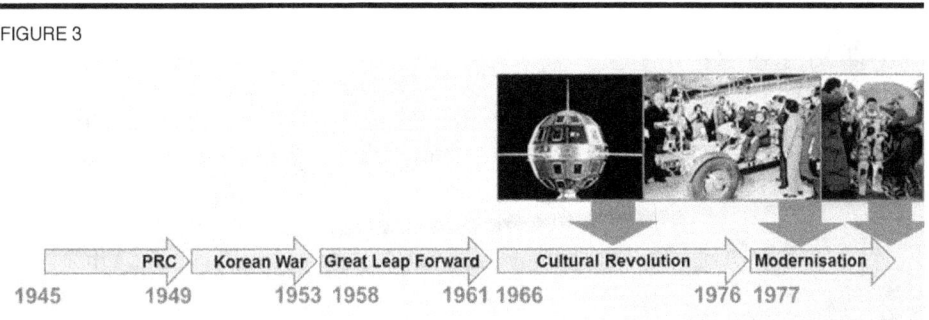

China's firsts in space are embedded in the dramatic decades of the nation's post-war development.

And they did!

In 1961, after the Great Leap Forward, the Chinese leadership focussed on the so-called "Four Modernizations," among which was science and technology. The satellite work group within the CAS was still struggling. The Director of CAS's Geophysical Institute, Zhao Jiuzhang, saw the big progress the military made with the development of missiles and wrote a letter to the party leaders in which he suggested to:

> … combine the tests of our ballistic missile program with launching a satellite, and get the benefit of hitting two birds with one stone.

In 1966, the 'Cultural Revolution' deeply impacted the Chinese society and shook its foundations. Intellectuals were targeted and scientific institutions became places of conflict and violence. Under those circumstances, CAS and other institutions involved in space developments asked the Communist Party to protect their institutions with the help of the military. Mao approved and since that moment the Chinese space program and the People's Liberation Army have been tied together and have remained in tandem until today.

After 12 years of hard work, impacted by economic and technical constraints and political and societal interference, China launched its first satellite DFH 1 on April 24, 1970 (in the middle of the chaos of the 'Cultural Revolution'). China thus became the fifth nation in the world to do so. The 173 kg (not 2 tons) singing satellite was more of a propaganda instrument than the starting point for a solid, sustainable science program.

For comparison: 1970 was the year when Lunochod 1 explored the Moon, Venera 7 soft-landed on Venus, and Apollo 13 was able to make it home to Earth.

China's second civilian satellite was launched in 1975, carrying some of the payloads originally intended for DFH 1.

Although most Chinese satellites even today are based on the DFH bus, the actual intention of the scientists and engineers to aim for a long-term program only began to evolve in the 1990s.

China's Firsts in Space: Geostationary Satellite

In March 1974 three young telegraph workers wrote a letter to the government pointing out to the Chinese leaders that positions in geostationary orbit can only be assured by actually placing an object there.

In 1976 Mao—shortly before he died—approved the project and China notified the ITU—International Telecommunication Union—that it was going to place a telecommunications satellite into geostationary orbit by 1980.

After the end of the 'Cultural Revolution' in 1976, Deng Xiaoping was responsible for education, science, and technology—one of the four 'modernizations' that he thought to be the most important.

Deng became famous in illustrating his idea in a 1978 meeting when he tried to persuade his comrades to go for a communications satellite program in this enthusiastic way:

> If we invite a good teacher to give a lecture in the Great Hall of the People only 10,000 people can hear it, but if the same teacher were to give that lecture on television, and everyone had the equipment to receive it, that's a classroom of unlimited size.

It was also decided to develop a cryogenic upper stage, which led to a delay in the overall program. At a certain point Deng wanted to buy a communications satellite from the U.S.A., however this initiative did not work out and the self-set deadline for a launch in 1980 was slipping.

As before with the Soviet Union, the insight prevailed that instead of relying on support from other countries, China has to find and go its own way:

> If we buy, we can buy one or two, but we can't

go on buying indefinitely. So, we have to do this ourselves.

In the second half of 1983, China accomplished the five major systems needed:

- Launch vehicle
- Satellite
- Launch site
- The tracking and telemetry equipment
- A network of ground stations.

On Jan. 29, 1984, the first launch failed because of problems with the cryogenic upper stage.

The second attempt on April 8, 1984 was more or less successful. Problems with overheating batteries were solved by adjusting the satellite's attitude.

To recapitulate: in 1984 the Salut-7 space station was operational and the third Space Shuttle was put into service.

It took China 10 years to become the 5th geostationary nation in the world.

China's Firsts in Space: Manned Space Program

The most patience went into the Chinese manned space flight program.

Back in 1966, a feasibility study investigated the option to use synergies from the first satellite program for a human spaceflight program. In 1970—the Cultural Revolution was in full swing—"Project 714," aimed at launching a Chinese astronaut by 1973, was approved. A first group of candidates was sent for training to Star City, near Moscow.

In 1971, Mao disbanded the astronaut group again:

We should take care of affairs here on Earth first, and deal with extraterrestrial matters a little later.

Deng Xiaoping, who after the Cultural Revolution was responsible for space activities, was interested in space applications, but officially closed the manned space project in 1976: China "should not participate in the space race" and instead we should "focus our energies on urgently needed practical satellite applications."

On March 23, 1983, U.S. President Ronald Reagan delivered his SDI speech. In China this speech led to discussions on what role science and technology should play in a country's national development.

Again, a letter was written. In the beginning of 1986, four senior scientists wrote to Deng Xiaoping, pointing out that China needs to make concentrated efforts in the area of technology and technological breakthroughs.

In April 1986, the legendary document, "An Outline for National High Technology Planning," the "Plan 863," was published, and in October of that same year, the plan was approved and budget allocated.

As was previously the case, the goal of the Chinese human spaceflight program was not to race with, or surpass other nations, but rather to stop the process of falling too far behind. China was in need of an ambitious project that would develop a national space industrial infrastructure and promote the education of the needed talent and specialists.

A debate over serious differences as to whether China should go for a space shuttle design or the space capsule technology, caused the delay of "Plan 863" for more than five years.

Finally, the Standing Committee of the Politburo approved the space station plan on Sept. 21, 1992, and declared that the Chinese Space Station (CSS) was to be the core of China's human spaceflight efforts.

Despite lessons from the past, in the mid-1990s, China considered purchasing a complete Soyuz spacecraft from Russia. After lengthy negotiations, the Chinese scientists and engineers only "got bits and pieces, here and there" from their Russian counterparts and, in the end, the Chinese experts realised once more that they had to do the bulk of the work themselves.

Although the launch vehicle, the Long March 2F (LM-2F), was ready in time, the Shenzhou capsule was behind schedule.

Only on Nov. 20, 1999, the unmanned Shenzhou 1 lifted off, followed by three more automated test flights.

Interestingly, the systems on the last unmanned mission, the Shenzhou 4 flight, were equipped to support a mission with two taikonauts who would spend three days in space. The flight of Yang Liwei with Shenzhou 5 on Oct. 15, 2003 was a one-crew mission that lasted 21 hours and made China the third country in the world capable of human spaceflight.[1]

---

1. For more on these historical aspects of China's first steps into space, it is highly recommended to study the paper by Gregory Kulacki and Jeffrey G. Lewis, "A Place for One's Mat: China's Space Program, 1956-2003." American Academy of Arts and Sciences, 2009.

Caesura—The Economic Boom

The economic success at the turn of the millennium not only provided China with the self-confidence and self-esteem to proffer big societal concepts, but was also the point in time to give science and technology—and with it space—a fundamental new orientation and direction to meet the needs of the future of the nation.

White Papers

Since 2001, in parallel with the respective five-year plans, China has issued its "White Papers on Space Activities." The prevailing tone of all White Papers has remained the same until today:

> The Chinese government has all along regarded the space industry as an integral part of the state's comprehensive development strategy, and upheld that the exploration and utilization of outer space should be for peaceful purposes and benefit the whole of mankind. ...
>
> The role of space activities in a country's overall development strategy is becoming increasingly salient, and their influence on human civilization and social progress is increasing.

> *The defined key principles for the development of space activities are:*
> - Maintain and serve the country's overall development strategy.
> - Uphold the policy of independence and self-reliance.
> - Maintain comprehensive, coordinated and sustainable development.
> - Adherence to the policy of opening up to the outside world.

> China's space strategy has three major characteristics:
> 1. *consistency,*
> 2. *consistency,* and
> 3. *consistency.*

The strategy at the highest level remains consistent, i.e. incremental progress is achieved step-by-step.

No giant leaps forward!

China is more than willing, indeed actively seeking, international cooperation.

Roadmap—A Schedule Up to the Year 2050

Additionally, the scientific community underwent a fundamental and tightly organized discussion on a roadmap for space science and space technology up to 2050. At the end of this process of stocktaking, analyzing, and evaluating the tasks for the future, the document *Space Science and Technology in China: A Roadmap to 2050* was published in 2009.

The *Roadmap 2050* analyzed the flaws and strengths of China's science community and the worldwide trends in space and technology, and came up with long-term and far-sighted goals and steps in achieving them.

The roadmap activity aimed at predicting the future developments of science and technology in accordance with the needs of the Chinese nation for the next 20-30 years,

> to address the needs of both the nation and society, the continued growth of economy and national competitiveness, the development of social harmony, and the sustainability between man and nature.

> *Furthermore, it was concluded that growth by purely extending the economic production has reached its limit!*

China's economic and social development will largely depend on science and technology through scientific discoveries, through the realization of so-called mega-projects (Beidou, High-Res Earth observation network, ground station network), and through new inventions and technological innovation.

The strategic aims of the roadmap reflect the principles of the White Papers.

And another conclusion was drawn during the roadmap process:

> The past 250 years' industrialization has resulted in the modernization and better-off life of less than 1 billion people, predominantly in Europe, North America, Japan, and Singapore. The next 50 years' modernization drive will definitely lead to an improved life for 2-3 billion people, including over 1 billion Chinese, doubling or tripling the economic increase over that of the past 250 years.

- For that, space will be one of the leading areas.
- *Space activities are encouraged and supported by the government;* important are *independence, self-reliance and self-renovation* while promoting *interna-*

FIGURE 4
Timeline of Shenzhou and Tiangong Missions

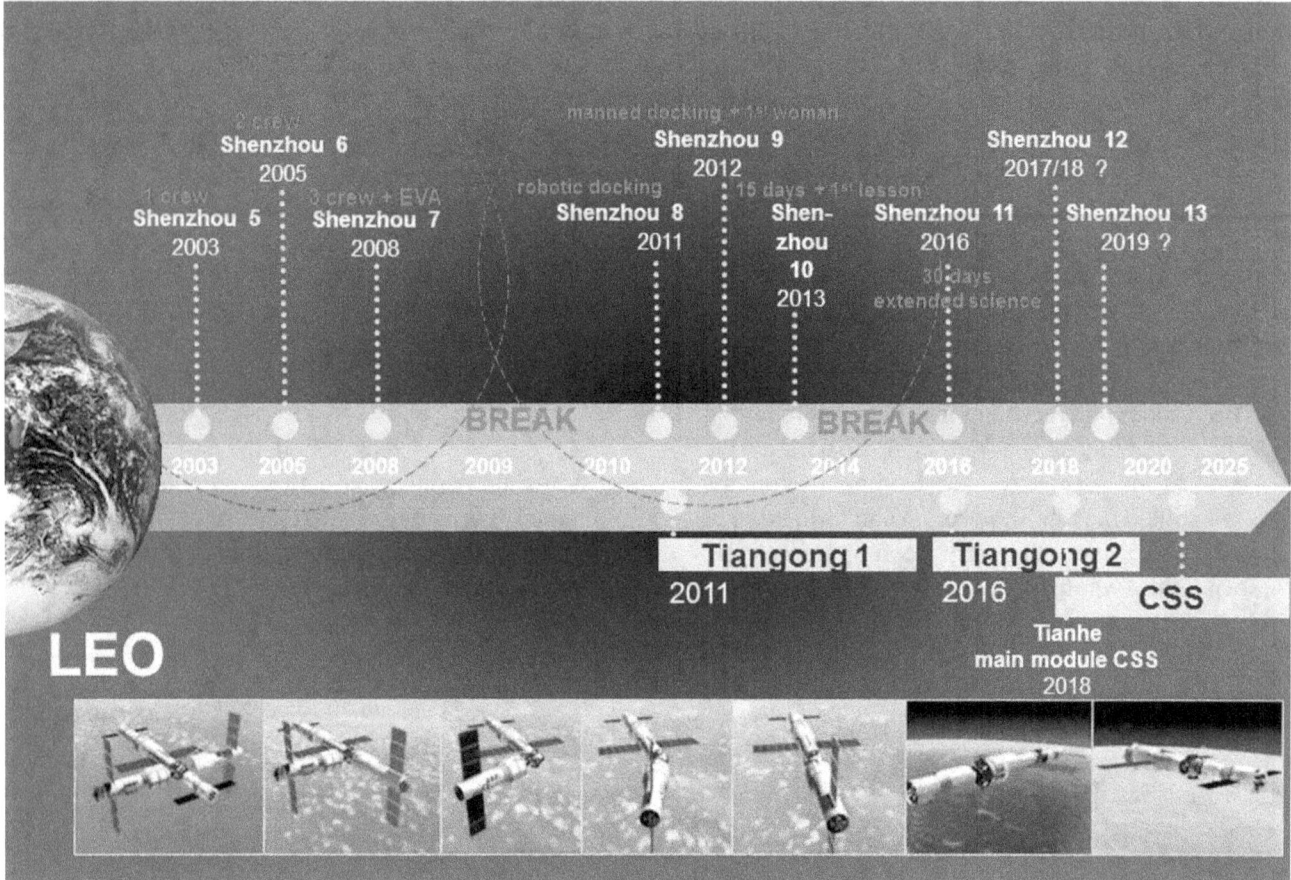

LEO—Efficiency Is Key

Is there a specific reason why the Chinese space program seems to be on a slower pace as compared to the leading space nations, the Soviet Union and U.S.A.?

In order to find an answer to this question, a closer look at China's Shenzhou program might be helpful.

The low number of manned missions is characterized by a specific approach.

In 2003 Shenzhou 5, with one person on board, was launched. Two years later saw the two-crew mission with Shenzhou 6, and 3 years later, a three-taikonaut crew conducted the first Chinese EVA on Shenzhou 7.

The space community expected that more missions would happen, however, what we observed was a 3-year break until 2011. We assume that this break was used to learn, analyze, and improve, before going on! China had to learn fundamental space technologies for its manned space program.

Also, the next three Shenzhou missions again formed a kind of cluster.

tional exchanges and cooperation; the modernization of space technology is combined with technology imports based on win-win deals.

- China *selects a limited number of projects that are of vital significance to the national economy and social development.*
- Space activities are evaluated according to economic efficiency criteria.
- China is sticking to *integrated planning* by combining long-term development and short-term development, combining spacecraft and ground equipment, and coordinating development of space technology, application and science.

China's space activities are *long-term, stable, and sustainable* development to benefit the strategy of *revitalizing the country* with *science and education and that of sustainable development*, as well as in economic construction, national security, science and technology development, and social progress.

FIGURE 5

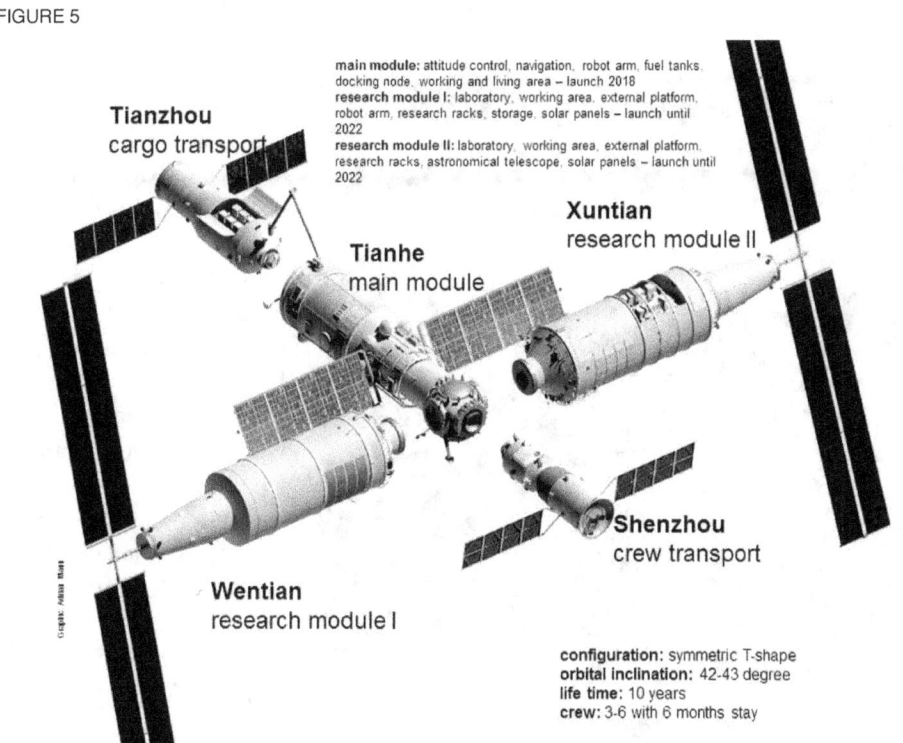

main module: attitude control, navigation, robot arm, fuel tanks, docking node, working and living area – launch 2018
research module I: laboratory, working area, external platform, robot arm, research racks, storage, solar panels – launch until 2022
research module II: laboratory, working area, external platform, research racks, astronomical telescope, solar panels – launch until 2022

Tianzhou cargo transport

Tianhe main module

Xuntian research module II

Shenzhou crew transport

Wentian research module I

configuration: symmetric T-shape
orbital inclination: 42-43 degree
life time: 10 years
crew: 3-6 with 6 months stay

Older conceptual illustration of the future Chinese Space Station (CSS), but it clearly emphasizes that the size will be manageable with indigenous capabilities.

In October 2011, the Shenzhou 8 craft performed an automatic rendezvous and docking with Tiangong 1. Only 7½ months later, Shenzhou 9 docked with TG-1. Among the three crew members was China's first female taikonaut. And again, one year later, in June 2013, the next Chinese human mission, Shenzhou 10, took place. Female crew-member Wang Yaping succeeded in fulfilling Deng Xiaoping's vision of a classroom of unlimited size when she delivered a lesson to 60 million Chinese students from space.

Again a three-year break took place, giving China time to learn, analyze, and improve what has been achieved so far. The last manned mission, a 30-day extended stay in space took place from October to November 2016.

And there is one more interesting efficiency fact to be noticed: Initially, Tiangong-1, 2, and 3 were planned. Since TG-1 could successfully fulfill many additional technology tests, many objec-

tives for Tiangong 2 were accomplished earlier. Once planned tests for Tiangong 3, such as a long-term stay in space, had been achieved already with TG-2, TG-3 became redundant and the assembly of the CSS will be initiated after TG-2.

Figure 5 shows an older conceptual illustration of the future Chinese Space Station (CSS). It is designed as a Mir-class orbital complex which, in full contrast to the International Space Station (ISS), can be operated and maintained within national space flight capacities.

What the observation of the Chinese space program has proven, is that time is not the main criterion for China—efficiency is. The diagram in Figure 6 illustrates that compared with the Soviet Union and the U.S.A., China has not been faster in the achievement of its firsts in space. However, China's strength and spe-

FIGURE 6

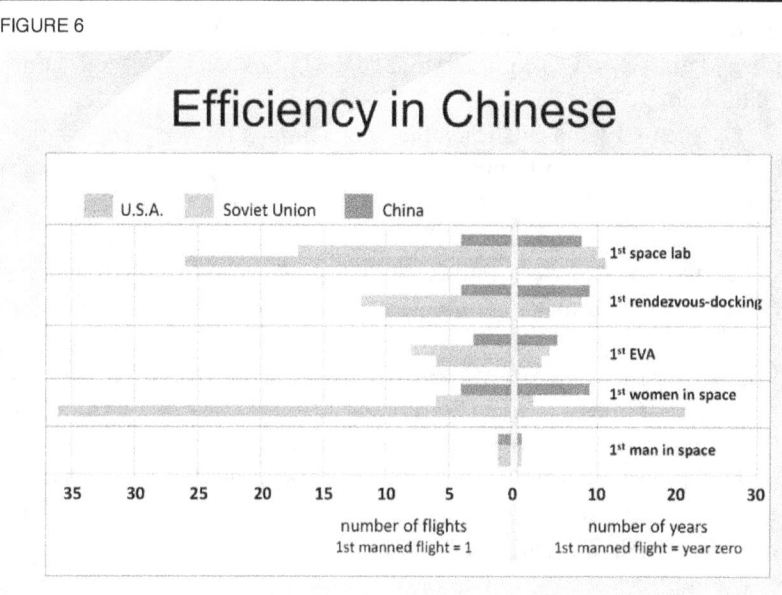

Efficiency in Chinese

U.S.A.   Soviet Union   China

1st space lab

1st rendezvous-docking

1st EVA

1st women in space

1st man in space

35   30   25   20   15   10   5   0   10   20   30

number of flights
1st manned flight = 1

number of years
1st manned flight = year zero

Efficiency in Chinese: Comparison of space achievements by the U.S.A., Soviet Union, and China.

FIGURE 7
Timeline of CLEP

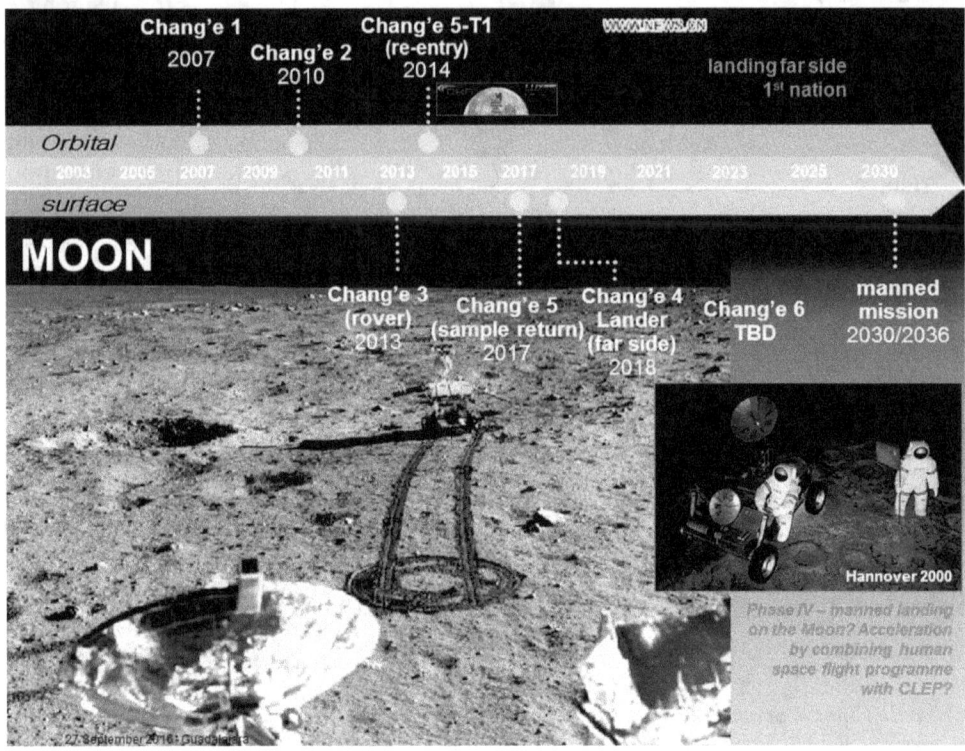

sponding resources have been established step-by-step.

Phase 1 started with the Chang'e 1 orbiter, orbiting the Moon and impacting at the end of the mission.

Chang'e 2, again an orbiter, flew an extended mission, reaching the Earth-Sun L2 Lagrange point and rendezvoused with asteroid Toutatis. Chang'e 2 is still active and supports tests for China's deep-space network.

Phase 2 started with the Chang'e 3 mission, comprising a Moon lander and the Yutu lunar rover. Then Chang'e 4 was expected. But China surprised the world.

Instead of Chang'e 4 (back-up of Chang'e 3), in preparation of Phase 3, Chang'e 5-T1—a test re-entry mission with Xiaofei, a downscaled Shenzhou capsule as re-entry body—was launched and returned to Earth, testing high-speed re-entry into the Earth's atmosphere.

And there was another surprise: The first commercial lunar payload—the Luxembourg-German 4M Manfred Memorial Moon Mission (with a *radio and dosimeter*) was on board of 5-T1.

We are now expecting in November the Chang'e 5 sample return mission, planned to bring 2 kg of Moon material to China.

Chang'e 4 will not end up in the museum; rather it will be repurposed with a new mission profile of landing on the far side of the Moon. There will be international and commercial cooperation for this mission. And China will write space history with the first ever landing of a human-made body on the lunar far side.

At this stage it might be fair to claim that China did very well in getting rid of its tortoise image.

cialty is its efficiency. The first woman in space, the first EVA, the first rendezvous-and-docking, the first space laboratory have been achieved with fewer flights as compared with the Soviet Union or the U.S.A.

For example, China achieved its first EVA during its third manned mission, while the Soviet Union accomplished this feat on its eighth flight and the U.S.A. on its sixth flight.

Or: the first female astronaut flew on China's fourth manned mission, while in the Soviet Union it was on the sixth national mission and in the U.S.A. it was on the 36th manned mission.

China might move slowly, but with respect to efficiency and performance, it is a global champion.

CLEP—China's Lunar Passing Lane

CLEP—China's Lunar Exploration Program—is China's test case for future deep-space exploration.

CLEP was planned in three phases—orbiter, lander, sample return mission. To each phase, two missions were assigned, allowing a step-wise build-up of capabilities: infrastructure, technology and resources.

The next phase can only start if the objectives of the previous phase have been accomplished and the corre-

Science on the Horizon—Mars and Beyond

Slowly but surely, China's space dream is beginning to embrace space science.

With respect to future space exploration, there is a firm focus on Mars. Chinese space experts are emphasizing that Mars exploration is based on the results and experiences of the lunar program. The engineering team from CLEP is involved in the Mars exploration project.

Having learned enormously from CLEP, China's first Mars mission goes bold: launching in 2020 with arrival at Mars in 2021, the Mars probe will accommodate lander, rover, and orbiter—all in one mission. If China succeeds, the tortoise image might be gone forever.

But already the recent Chinese science missions have earned worldwide respect. In December 2015, the dark matter particle explorer **DAMPE-Wukong** was launched. April 2016 saw the **Shijian 10** retrievable science satellite and August 2016 the **QUESS-Mozi** project, testing quantum communication.

For the near future, more and highly ambitious missions are in the pipeline:
- **HXMT**, a hard X-ray telescope
- **SMILE** for the observation of solar activities and space weather
- **MIT** for Magnetosphere-Ionosphere research
- **WCOM** for remote sensing of soil and oceans
- **ASO-S**, a Solar Observatory
- **Einstein** for the investigation of black holes
- **Missions to Jupiter** and/or **asteroids**.

Political Context: BRICS, SCO, and One Belt One Road

Space and politics are not always best friends but there is no denying that they interfere with each other.

Next to Brazil, Russia, India, and South Africa, China is one of the BRICS member states—an association of emerging economic powers finding its place in a multi-polar world.

While in 2015 the option of a joint BRICS space station was briefly discussed, there is now a realistic cooperation project in the area of Earth observation under way. Igor Komarov, Director of Roscomos State Corporation, explained in May 2016:

> The practical initiative, on which we are now working together with the BRICS countries, is a data exchange in distanced probing of the Earth, which will help in quicker responses to emergency situations, natural calamities, pollution and other aspects. I believe, it will find rather

prompt and very important practical use for the BRICS countries.

I would also like to point to the existence of the Shanghai Cooperation Organization (SCO). As the biggest regional organization, its objectives are comparable to the Helsinki Accords/Organization for Security and Cooperation in Europe (OSCE). SCO and BRICS are important for the China-led New Silk Road Economic Belt and Maritime Silk Road (One Belt One Road, OBOR): a mega-project of economic and societal development, aiming at the revitalization of the ancient Eurasian Silk Road model to create a bridge between Asia and Europe.

"The Belt and Road is China's initiative, but it belongs to the world. The idea came from China, but the benefits will flow to all countries." stressed China's Minister for Foreign Affairs Wang Yi, when he pointed to the Belt and Road Forum for International Cooperation that China is hosting in Beijing in May 2017.

One Belt One Road will be supported by the Digital Silk Road. Comprehensive space infrastructure—like the Chinese Beidou satellite navigation system and the Russian GLONASS—are ready to feed space applications, essential for the realization of the One Belt One Road endeavor. At this moment it is hard to predict how big the market for OBOR space applications will become, but it is certain that it will be enormous.

The One Belt One Road initiative is also complementary to the Eurasian Trade Zone, an initiative by Russian President Vladimir Putin. On several occasions he confirmed: "For us, China is a key partner in the region."

Embedded in the strategic environment for open international cooperation is the Chinese initiative within the frame of the United Nations. In March 2016, the United Nations Office for Outer Space Affairs (UNOOSA) and the China Manned Space Agency (CMSA) signed a framework agreement and a funding agreement to develop the space capabilities of UN member states via opportunities on board China's future space station.

China offers to UNOOSA member states:
- The use of the CSS for experiment payloads or joint research
- The development of modules, subsystems, components, or other platforms
- To train and to fly astronauts
- To share technical know-how.

FIGURE 8
China's Proposals for UNOOSA's Human Space Technology Initiative (HSTI)

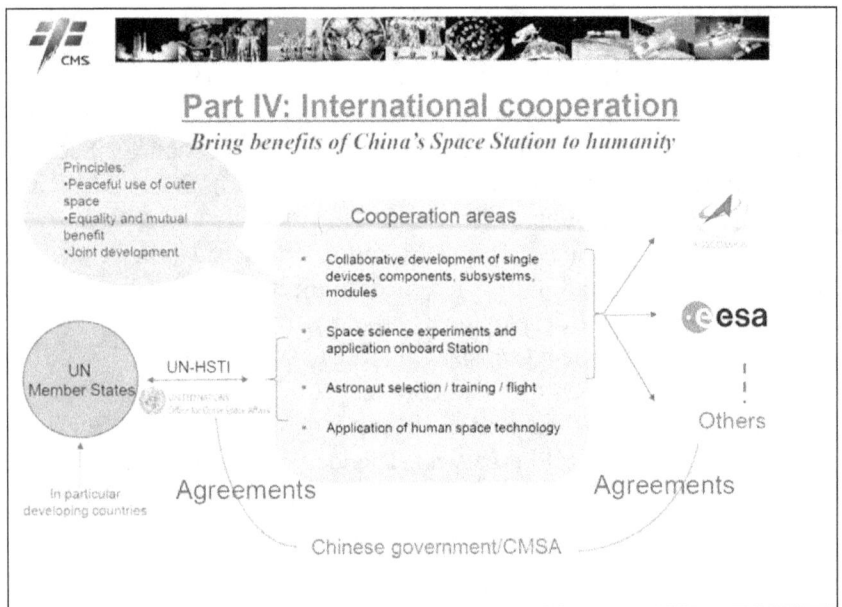

China's first taikonaut, Yang Liwei, stressed on April 24, 2016—when China first celebrated its national space day:

> Payload has been reserved in the Chinese space station, due to enter service around 2022, for international projects and foreign astronauts. Upon request, China will also train astronauts for other countries, and jointly train astronauts with the European Space Agency.... The future of space exploration lies in international cooperation. It's true for us, and for the United States too. China will not rule out cooperating with any country, and that includes the United States.

It might be that the Chinese Space Station has the potential to become the World's Space Station.

How the Future Might Look

Predictions about the future of the Chinese space program are rare. The authors of this paper are part of the Sino-European GoTaikonauts! team, which has closely observed China's space efforts for the last decade. Having seen its dyna-mism, inspiration, modesty, and perseverance, each one of us was looking at China's space dream from a different angle and dared to make predictions for its future development (see Figure 9). Although we are all convinced that Chinese space activities will increase and grow, we diverge a little bit on the speed and pace of how this will happen. However, we do agree that we will see China becoming the second space power after the United States.

The **science**-based considerations (red) say: Space exploration will remain important in China. The efforts will continue to grow linear because space science and technology is considered to be a tool for the development of the overall society. Space is a fundamental desire of mankind. It has the image of being a high-tech area. It is extremely difficult and by challenging space, any society can demonstrate its capabilities.

The **societally** focussed opinion (blue) says: Space exploration in China will remain important, but other issues (climate change, energy, social welfare, infrastructure projects—also on a global/Asian/African scale) will require more resources. Once the creation of a harmonious, possibly global, society is achieved,

FIGURE 9

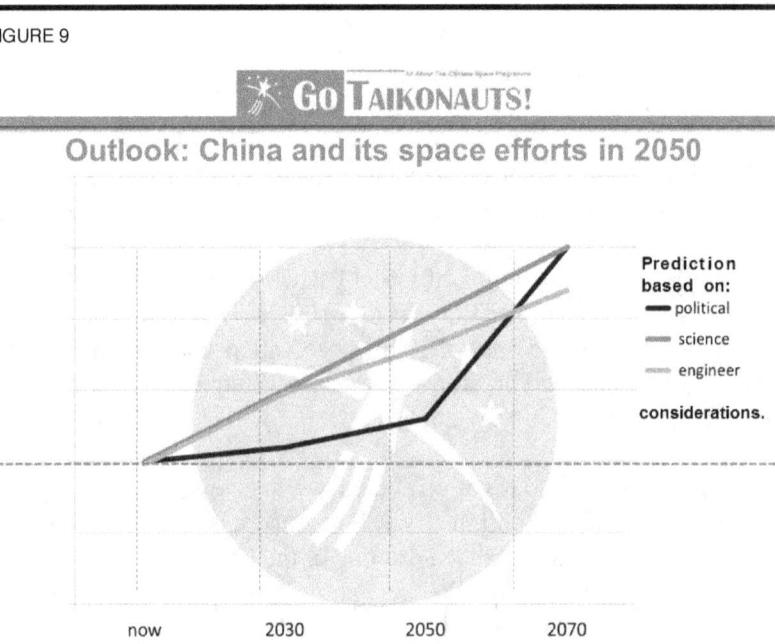

Predictions for the future development of China's space program.

space exploration will experience a renaissance.

The **engineering** considerations (green) say: China has a good track record to complete its space plans, which have been demonstrated in the manned space flight, lunar exploration, Beidou navigation system, and other civil and military programs. So it is very reasonable to see that China will continue its fast expansion in space, but with a pace consistent with the slightly slowed down growth rate of its economy. Although there are many challenges ahead, we will see China become the second space power after the United States.

China's Space Program Is Neither Hare nor Tortoise

In the beginning, it has been slow. However, if the frame is set and decisions are taken, things speed up and the tortoise might convert into a hare.

Leaps forward are possible and will advance the whole process. Leap-frogging is a Chinese specialty.

And something else is characteristic of China's

FIGURE 10

Neither hare nor tortoise—China has its own pace of space.

space program:

A guest in a Chinese restaurant is often taken by surprise when studying the gigantic menu. The trick is: a set of basic components can be combined for an almost unlimited number of dishes. China's space program often works in the same way.

So, the next time you sit in a Chinese restaurant, please think of the Chinese space program … frogs and frogs.

Note

This article is a summary of the IAC2016 paper (IAC-16,E3,2,5-E3.2-29th IAA Symposium on Space Policy, Regulations and Economics) with the same title. For better detail, please, consult the paper.

Acknowledgement

This paper would not have been possible without the year-long exchange with, and inspiration of GoTaikonauts! team member and author Chen Lan.

References

1. G. Kulacki, J. G. Lewis, A Place for One's Mat: China's Space Program, 1956-2003, American Academy of Arts and Sciences 2008, ISBN: 0-87724-079-5.

2. G. Kulacki, Why China is Building a Space Station, June 2012, Union of Concerned Scientists (accessed June 2016).

3. B. Harvey, China in Space—The Great Leap Forward (2013), ISBN: 9781461450436, 9781461450429

4. W. Carey, No Giant Leap—A Review of China's Space Activities White Papers (2000-2011), *GoTaikonauts!—All about the Chinese space program*, 4 (2012) 25-29.

5a. Information Office of the State Council of the People's Republic of China. November 2000, China's Space Activities in 2000 (accessed June 2016).

5b. Information Office of the State Council of the People's Republic of China. October 2006, China's Space Activities in 2006 (accessed June 2016).

5c. Information Office of the State Council of the People's Republic of China. December 29, 2011, China's Space Activities in 2016 (accessed June 2016).

6. W. Carey, J. Myrrhe, What if…? Searching for Evidence—An Attempt to Analyse the 'Space Science & Technology in China: A Roadmap to 2050,' *GoTaikonauts!—All about the Chinese space program*, 12 (2014) 31-38.

7. H. Guo, J. Wu, Space Science & Technology in China: A Roadmap to 2050, Science Press Beijing, ISBN 978-7-03-025703-1, Springer ISBN 978-3-642-05341-2, 2010.

8. ISU SSP03 Tracks to Space—Report, ISU Strasbourg (accessed June 2016).

9. Ji QiMing, Chinese Space Station CSS and International Cooperation, 57th session of the Committee on the Peaceful Uses of Outer Space—COPUOS, Vienna, 11-20 June 2014.

10. Xinhua, April 24, 2016 (accessed June 2016).

Worldwide Spirit of Optimism Over the New Silk Road!

At the conference on the centenary of the German-American space pioneer Krafft Ehricke on March 25, 2017 in Munich, Helga Zepp-LaRouche gave the following address.

The beauty of the Chinese music[1] has, I hope, put us in the right mood to think about and celebrate Krafft Ehricke's birthday. Krafft Ehricke is without a doubt—in my humble opinion—one of the greatest Germans who ever lived. That is because he developed a vision of where mankind can go, and I consider it a very great privilege to have been able to get to know him personally.

In 1982 I had the opportunity to give several presentations with him in various German cities, and I can confirm from personal experience the picture of him which his daughter Krista has drawn of him so incredibly lovingly.[2] He was an incredible humanist, vastly educated in Classical culture; he was a genius so bubbling with ideas that it was really one of the high points of my life to have known such a personality. Fortunately, several of his presentations are available as videos on the Internet, and I urge you all to become acquainted with him yourselves.[3]

EIRNS/Christopher Lewis

Helga Zepp-LaRouche

I am also positive that if Krafft Ehricke were with us today, he would be incredibly optimistic that his vision, which was often contested in his lifetime, is going to be realized. It wasn't just his vision, but the overall continuation of space exploration, that ran up against objections and resistance. He would recognize that we actually have the strategic constellation today to realize his vision in the near future. We have already heard about the Chinese space program, which is perhaps the "frog" that leaps[4] because the Chinese have a vision of mining helium-3 from the far side of the Moon to fuel a future fusion economy on Earth. That goal has also been discussed by the European Space Agency, but I believe that China is educating the most scientists and researchers in the area of space exploration worldwide, and therefore I am optimistic that this "leap-frogging" will definitely proceed.

Look at the collaboration of the BRICS nations in the area of space exploration: It was mentioned that India has already carried out a successful Mars mission, and, as Prime Minister Modi said, it was done at a tenth of the cost that NASA needed. There are unbelievable developments underway.

---

1. Immediately before the beginning of Zepp-LaRouche's address, Feride Istogu-Gillesberg had performed a Chinese love song.

2. Earlier a message of greeting from Krafft Ehricke's daughter Krista Ehricke had been read to the conference.

3. See "Krafft Ehricke on the Extraterrestrial Imperative" **[in German]**, https://www.youtube.com/watch?v=9UznFry-Y9s and Krafft Ehricke,

"Lunar Industrialization & Settlement—Birth of Polyglobal Civilization" **[in English]**, https://www.youtube.com/watch?v=-ZuSnPgHnjs

4. Jacqueline Myrrhe, in her earlier speech on the development of the Chinese space program, had posed the question, whether it is like the tortoise or the hare, and ultimately compared it to the frog, which reaches its goal in huge leaps.

Krafft Ehricke's idea that the exploration and colonization of space is an evolutionary necessity, without which mankind cannot survive in the long term, is the other point. It's not an option, not a matter of choice; we must do it because in two billion years, at the latest, our Sun will not be so pleasant, and thus we must have found other solutions before that time.

But the most important thing about Krafft Ehricke, the reason why he is so enormously relevant today and important, is that his vision, and space exploration as a whole, implies the idea of an open world, that the world is not a closed system with limited resources, but an integral part of the Universe, and that human creativity is a creative, physical force in this Universe.

Epochal Change

I maintain that we are now experiencing an epochal change, in which this idea is beginning to assert itself—that is, a revolution in worldview is in process. You have certainly not observed this if you only watch "Sonntags-Stammtisch" on Bavarian Radio, or read *Bild-Zeitung* or *Spiegel* or the *FAZ*, but that does not mean that it is not reality. This is my thesis: We currently have an epochal change underway, which is no less fundamental than the transition from the Middle Ages to the Modern Age.

Just briefly bring to mind the axiomatics of the Middle Ages—the axioms of the scholastics, the peripatetics, superstition, and so on—and then came a Renaissance, the Italian Renaissance of the Fifteenth Century, created by thinkers such as Nicholas of Cusa and Brunelleschi, a revival of Plato's works which had been totally forgotten in Europe for 1700 years.

With the Renaissance came a totally new worldview, which understood the individual and the role of man totally differently, but also laid the basis for the emergence of modern science, Classical art, sovereign nation states, and similar developments, which have nourished us for the past 600 years.

We are now experiencing just such an epochal change, perhaps one even more dramatic, and I dare to predict that all the axioms associated with this old paradigm will land in the dustbin of history—the idea of limits to growth; the neoliberal idea that money is wealth; that man only represents a burden on the environment, and the fewer people, the better; the neoconservative idea of geopolitics, that foreign policy must always be a zero-sum game, in which, if one wins, the other loses. All of these ideas will go into the dustbin and a new paradigm will be established, namely, the ideal of a united mankind. And mankind, at least in large part, is now establishing a common ground of reason in which the common aims of mankind are placed before national interests.

There are currently two essential dynamics in which this new view is being realized.

One is—as I will discuss at length later on—China's policy of the New Silk Road, which has become, within three and a half years, the largest infrastructure program in the history of mankind. It already involves 70 nations and 4.5 billion people. It is already 12 times greater than the Marshall Plan of the post-World War II period, and has unlimited growth potential.

This new paradigm of the One Belt, One Road Initiative (or the New Silk Road) has already led to unprecedented optimism among many peoples of the world. For example, in Africa, people for the first time have a justified hope that they will soon be able to overcome their underdevelopment with China's help.

Precisely because this new paradigm is based on win-win cooperation—where one nation, China, admittedly benefits, but the other cooperating nations profit just as much—it is the basis for world peace in the long run. This is because it is in the interests of every state to have others develop, otherwise one's own development is jeopardized.

The New U.S. Presidency

The second dynamic which gives cause for optimism—and this will surprise quite a few of you and quite a few will not agree with me at first. But I ask your indulgence because I must enter into the degradation of American politics: The second dynamic is Donald Trump's election victory. I would really ask you, for a start, to forget everything that you have read in *Bild-Zeitung* on page 2, because that is psychological warfare; it is black propaganda of the sort that is only used against the enemy in the time of war. The representatives of the collapsing paradigm, the neoliberal paradigm—the media, the intelligence services, and the British Empire—are conducting total war against President Trump.

I would like to address just a few aspects of his latest speeches, given in Michigan, Tennessee, Kentucky, and Washington, in which he made an emphatic call for the United States to return to the "American System" of economy. He especially referenced the first Republican President, Abraham Lincoln who, as a young candidate for Congress at the age of 23, in 1832, promoted the building of a railroad in America, although he had never even seen a steam engine at that time. Thirty years later, as President, he signed the law for the building of the Transcontinental Railroad, which linked the east and west coasts of the United States.

In a similar way, Trump cited President Eisenhower who, as an officer after the First World War, travelled in a military convoy along the Lincoln Highway across the country. This made such an impression on him that 30 years later, he signed the law establishing the Interstate Highway system. Then Trump said: We need the American System again today, the policy of George Washington, Alexander Hamilton, Henry Clay, and Lincoln.

Most people don't know what this American System is, but it was the fundamental American idea in opposition to the British Empire.

There are other ideas that Trump has mentioned—that he wants to invest a trillion dollars in infrastructure, that he doesn't want to wage any more wars of intervention such as Bush and Obama did, that he wants to put relations with Russia and China on the basis of cooperation, and others. These are the basic goals—such as peace with Russia and China—that everyone in Germany should be glad about, and say: Finally there is hope that this danger of war can be overcome!

But then where does this unbelievable agitation come from? Why is the whole Establishment in such a state of shock? Although Trump was elected four months ago, a war is now being waged against him by Hillary Clinton, the Democratic Party, and the neocons. They have invented a so-called narrative—a narrative or a concoction of lies—as to why Hillary Clinton lost the election, which says she did not lose because she represents the paradigm which leaves a large portion of the people behind, or because she was too arrogant to even travel to campaign among the "deplorables" in the Rust Belt. But rather, that Trump won the election because Putin helped him do so, by having Russian hackers tamper with Democratic Party emails.

What is naturally omitted is what was in the emails—namely, that the Democratic Party put Bernie Sanders at a disadvantage and gave preference to Hillary Clinton entirely illegally, and also the speech that Hillary gave to the Wall Street bankers, which only then was made known.

But several members of the intelligence community, the whistleblowers—such as William Binney, who developed the NSA surveillance program and thus knows exactly how it functions—have said: No, it is totally clear that if it was Russian hacking, the NSA could have identified the server from which it came with no problem. But these are *leaks*—that is, the disclosure of classified information to the public—and the question is, who could have done it.

The U.S. intelligence services have very obviously concocted dossiers on Trump, with the aid of British intelligence—and not just former MI6 agent Christopher Steele—that were then leaked to the public. The possibility that the British equivalent of the NSA, the GCHQ, did the work for the American intelligence services is now also being investigated.

Congress is now investigating everything, and the chairman of the House Intelligence Committee, Devin Nunes, has just said that there is so far only one visible *bona fide* criminal act, and that is the illegal release of information—and not some hacking. If you read *Bild-Zeitung*, you read exactly the opposite—that a Watergate is underway and the like. But that will be further investigated. Nunes will hold a closed hearing with the cooperation of the NSA and the non-cooperation of the FBI and CIA.

A few days ago, a leading journalist from a public broadcaster told me that there is an internal watchword that no program on Trump may be presented without the inclusion of derogatory remarks.

Where does this whole dynamic come from? Is it, as the French intelligence services suspected after Trump's election, that the old Establishment is afraid of losing its privileges, and thus its income stream? Or is there a deeper cause? Obviously I am of the second view, that the conflict concerns what Friedrich List—the German economist who spent several years in America—identified in his time as the total conflict between the "British System of Economy" and the "American System of Economy." The British system is based on free trade, buying cheap and selling dear, control of raw materials, the cheapest possible labor force, the least possible social support, and control of trade.

Contrasted to that is the American System, which actually goes back to Alexander Hamilton—the idea that the real source of wealth is the creativity of the

FIGURE 1

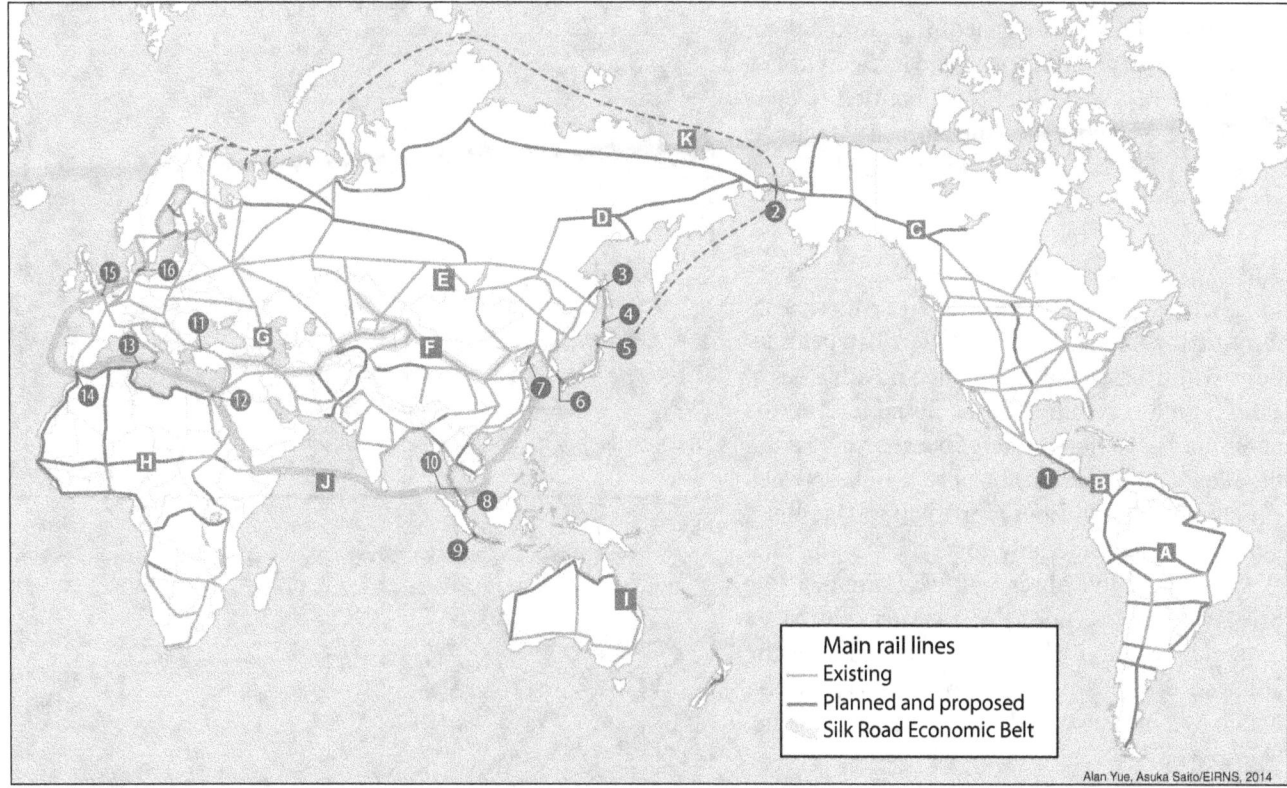

The infrastructure corridors of the Schiller Institute's proposed World Land-Bridge.

labor force, and that therefore an economy requires the defense of the internal market with protectionist measures, and the maximum development of its own labor force.

The American System also includes the national bank, created by Alexander Hamilton, and a credit system dedicated to the general welfare, which includes investments in the real economy, such as infrastructure and scientific and technological progress, with the goal of raising productivity. That is exactly the policy that was carried out by Washington, Alexander Hamilton, John Quincy Adams, Lincoln, and Franklin D. Roosevelt, and to which Trump just now explicitly referred.

You should remember: The American Revolution, or the American War of Independence, was fought against the British Empire, with the goal of achieving the right of Americans to have their own manufactures, a right which their colonial master had denied. And the British Empire has never gotten over the loss of its most important colonies, namely those in America, but has constantly tried with all means at its disposal to reverse this process, first through the War of 1812; then through the Civil War against Lincoln, during which Britain was tacitly allied with the southern states, and which was also financed by the British interest—General Lee got money directly from banks in Boston and Philadelphia [that financed the cotton trade for Britain].

After the British lost the Civil War against Lincoln, they considered it impossible to win the United States back militarily, but they now had to try subversion, in other words, the "open conspiracy" (as H.G. Wells called it) to persuade the American establishment to create a unipolar world on the basis of the "Anglo-American Special Relationship"—a *world empire*. That was the case between Churchill and Truman, Bush senior and Thatcher, Blair and Bush junior, and Cameron and Obama.

In Germany this subject is as little known as is the fact that Bismarck developed the German economy from a feudal state to an industrial nation within a few years on the basis of the American System of economy, because he had learned the theories of Henry C. Carey. This was due to the fact that the head of the German Industrial Association at the time, Wilhelm von Kardorff, was a fierce advocate of Friedrich List and Henry Carey; he took the example of American industrialization under Lincoln as a model for the transformation of Germany. He then wrote a small but very readable book entitled, *Gegen den Strom* [Against the Current], in which the difference between the American and British systems is very well explained.

The New Silk Road

There is also a dynamic that, if America returns to its roots and wants, above all, to put relations with Russia and China on a positive basis, essentially everything will be possible. And the potential is absolutely there, because, as I said, the New Silk Road is not only a link between Chongqing and Duisburg, or Yiwu to Hamburg, but there is considerably more in the pipeline. We are not passive observers. We claim the New Silk Road also as "our baby," because it is based on the conception which we proposed after the collapse of the Soviet Union in 1991, and on which we have worked for the past 26 years. [**Figure 1**]

The New Silk Road Becomes the World Land-Bridge—that's the name of a study which we have published in English, Arabic, and Chinese—and which will very soon be published in German. And if you look at how this concept, which Xi Jinping presented for the first time in Kazakhstan in 2013, has exploded over the past three and a half years, then you can see that a total transformation is underway.

Part of the Silk Road [**Figure 2**] is the "Maritime Silk Road of the 21st Century" in the tradition of Admiral Zheng He, who travelled from the Asian Pacific to Venice and to Africa in the 15th Century. Today the ports of all of these Asian states are linked to each other, and further, are linked to Hamburg and Rotterdam. The Silk Road includes six economic corridors. More than 70 nations comprising 4.4 billion people are taking part, and $21 trillion in investments are planned.

The corridors are growing rapidly. This [**Figure 3**] is an arrangement among China, Mongolia, and Russia, decided upon during the 2016 meeting of the Shanghai Cooperation Organization, that encompasses 32 projects. These [**Figure 4**] are the Silk Road trains going daily from Chinese cities such as Yiwu, Xi'an, and Chongqing, to Duisburg, Lyon, Hamburg, and Rotter-

FIGURE 2

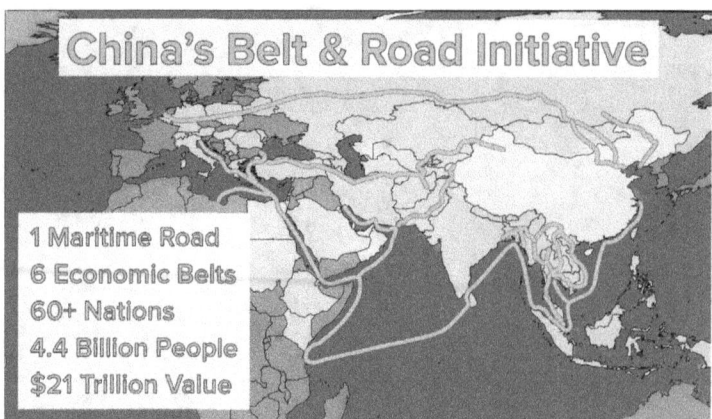

The corridors of the Belt and Road initiative at sea and on land.

FIGURE 3

The economic corridor China-Mongolia-Russia.

dam. A train travels daily from Chongqing to Europe.

This [**Figure 5**] was the original idea for linking China with Central and West Asian countries; this [**Figure 6**] is a corridor through Bangladesh, India, China, and Myanmar, which means a total transformation of this region of the world; this [**Figure 7**] is the New Eurasian Land-Bridge.

There are also several components of the Silk Road that are growing insanely fast.

For Africa, this development is a total novelty, because the banks which China and the BRICS countries founded, were created with the explicit aim of compensating for the lack of investment in infrastructure by the IMF, World Bank, and others over the last decades; these new banks are exclusively for investment in infrastructure, not speculation.

About four weeks ago, Ethiopia's first railroad—

FIGURE 4

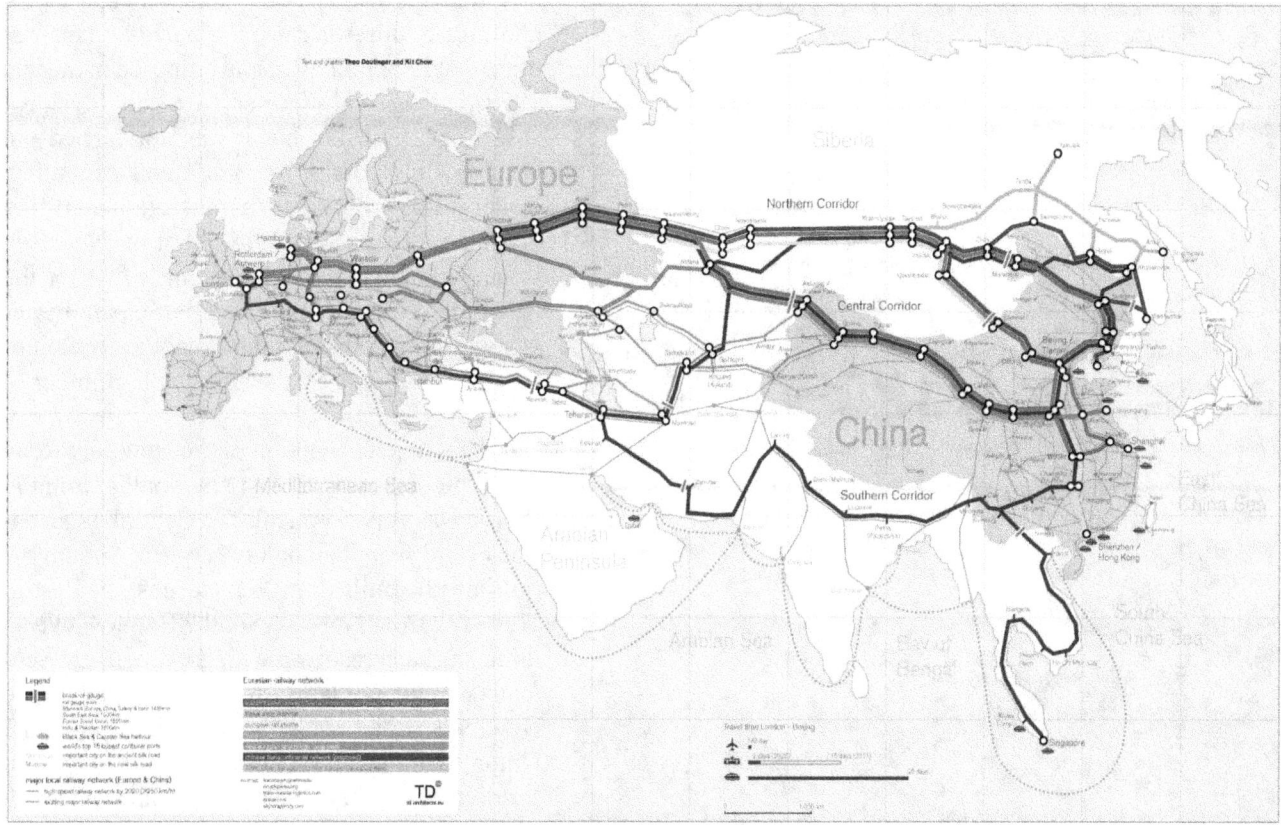

The already existing lines of the "Iron Silk Road", on which regular freight trains run between China and Europe on a daily basis.

from the capital Addis Ababa to Djibouti—went into operation; it was ready to go last fall, but was then tested and upgraded with security measures. Meanwhile another railroad is under construction, from Rwanda to Uganda to the Congo.

Here [**Figure 8**] is another project, Transaqua, which Lyndon LaRouche and the Schiller Institute have campaigned for, for 40 years. It was originally developed by Italian engineers, and the idea is that man can reverse the drying-up of Lake Chad. Lake Chad has dried up to about 10 percent of its original capacity. You can redirect unused water-flow from the Congo region, at approximately 500 meters altitude—not only the actual waters of the Congo River, but the Congo's tributaries—through a river and canal system into Lake Chad, and thus create arable production through irrigation for twelve adjacent states, and thereby begin the industrialization of Africa.

This project was recently surveyed for the first time

FIGURE 5

The economic corridor of China-Central- and -West Asia along the historic Silk Road.

by a Chinese firm, Power China, the same firm that made the Three Gorges Dam a reality. A feasibility study is now under way, and that will lead very soon to allowing 100 billion cubic meters of water to flow into

FIGURE 6

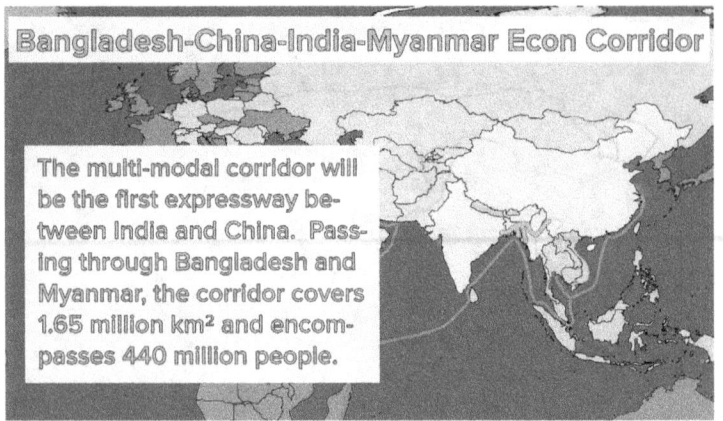

Bangladesh-China-India-Myanmar Econ Corridor

The multi-modal corridor will be the first expressway between India and China. Passing through Bangladesh and Myanmar, the corridor covers 1.65 million km² and encompasses 440 million people.

The economic corridor Bangladesh-China-India-Myanmar.

FIGURE 7

New Eurasian Land-Bridge

With the New Eurasian Land-Bridge route goods from central China are reaching Western Europe in 2 to 3 weeks (rather than 5 weeks by ocean). By mid-2016 over 2,000 rail shipments had already occurred.

Lake Chad per year.

This [**Figure 9**] is the comprehensive program for South America. The blue line is a program that Lyndon LaRouche proposed in the late 1970s, along with former Mexican President José López Portillo, but it was not carried out because of sabotage by Brazil and Argentina. But now this proposal for a transcontinental "Bi-oceanic railroad" to Peru is part of the New Silk Road. One positive development is that for the first time, Germany will also participate by investing in the construction of another stretch of the rail in Bolivia. So that is a small glimmer of light.

The whole conception of the New Silk Road has exploded over the last six months. Initially Russia was very skeptical. The Central Asian nations were skeptical, or have argued, Should the rail lines be built from West to East, or East to West—or from North to South? But now everything has been resolved with good will. On September 2 and 3 of last year, the integration of the New Silk Road with the Eurasian Economic Union took place at a huge economic forum in Vladivostok, where Japan also joined in, with huge investments in the Russian Far East. This process advanced at the G20 Summit in Hangzhou at the beginning of September, then advanced further at the ASEAN meeting in Laos.

FIGURE 8

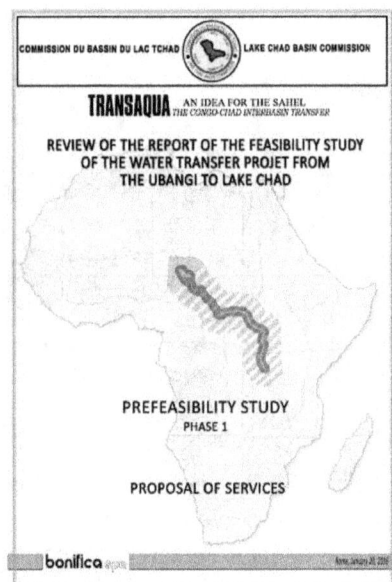

The Transaqua project, developed by the Italian engineering firm Bonifica, is intended to reverse the drying out of Lake Chad, and its feasibility is now being studied by the Chinese hydraulic engineering concern, Power China.

FIGURE 9

The infrastructure corridors proposed for Latin America by Lyndon LaRouche at the end of the 1970s (blue), and the projects proposed by China today (red).

China clearly took leadership of this process as early as the G20 Summit, at which it said that it wanted to immediately base the world economy on innovation, and to enlist the developing countries in scientific and technological breakthroughs, so that their development will no longer be delayed. China has declared its intention to overcome poverty on the entire planet by the year 2025.

The process advanced further at the Asia-Pacific Economic Cooperation (APEC) meeting in Lima, Peru in November of last year, and now even some western think tanks have realized that their former negative evaluation is no longer appropriate. For example, PricewaterhouseCoopers produced a comprehensive study in which it said that at present the Chinese economy is the locomotive of the world economy, and will remain so. *Forbes Magazine* has had about seven relatively objective articles on the range of projects. This is an unstoppable dynamic, it says.

And, as I said, President Trump has invited President Xi Jinping to his estate of Mar-a-Lago in Florida on April 6-7, and there is every indication that the Chinese are prepared to make huge investments in the construction of U.S. infrastructure. There was a conference in Hongkong at which Chinese economists said that America's infrastructure deficit is not one trillion dollars, but eight trillion. Japan has already said that it wants to participate with $150 billion in the development of American high-speed rail. China has said many times—for example, Deputy Foreign Minister Madame Fu Ying, the most important woman in China, has said it—that the Silk Road can be the bridge between America and the Eurasian Silk Road, through development of American infrastructure.

Thus there are very, very hopeful events in process.

A Question of the Image of Man

Why is this so enormously important?

The entire trans-Atlantic world has been dominated over the last decades by the paradigm of closed systems and zero growth. Take a step back: In the 1950s and 60s, it was perfectly self-evident that poverty in the Third World would be overcome somehow. Then there were the UN Development Decades, in which we would set goals for ten years at a time, then for the next ten years, in order to finally and totally eliminate poverty and underdevelopment on this planet.

But this normal, humanistic orientation was discontinued by a whole array of propaganda measures. Probably the most serious was the publication of the Club of Rome's book *Limits to Growth* in 1972. Authors Forrester and Meadows simply determined a desired result, and then programmed their computer model so it came out exactly that way. They used linear equations to get this result, and perpetrated an absolute swindle: They completely left out the idea of scientific and technological progress, and the resulting redefinition of raw materials and production methods.

With great fanfare, this book was translated and distributed in all languages, and presented this basic idea: The world was developing up until 1971, and now we have reached a point of equilibrium; we approached it asymptotically, and now we must be sustainable. Now we must conserve; above all, we must conserve energy, and there will be no more technological progress, but rather "appropriate technology"—which is then translated as no technology.

With this went the idea that we are an Earth-bound system, and that overpopulation is the greatest problem, because people are actually parasites who are a burden on the environment, and the less people, the better.

Now these were not totally new ideas, because this issue was implicitly the subject of the American Revolution. In 1751 Benjamin Franklin wrote an essay entitled, *Observations Concerning the Increase of Mankind,*[5] in which he argued this: The more people there are, the better, because each person brings his own creative potential with him to human society, and thus enriches society overall. Thomas Malthus, who wrote *An Essay on the Principle of Population,*[6] embodied the opposite view; as is well known, he had the idea that the numbers of people increase faster than the improvements in agriculture needed to sustain them, and thus the population must always be reduced. And just like all the other British economists—Adam Smith, Jeremy Bentham, John Stuart Mill, David Ricardo—he worked for the British East India Company, which earned its riches through trading in slaves and opium.

Therefore, what was really at issue—then, and especially now—is the image of man. Lyndon LaRouche has written a great deal about that. I would like you to read my husband's articles, because he has worked out in the clearest way where mankind's creative potential lies. In contrast to all other living species and animals, which are also intelligent, man is the only species which can

5. *Observations Concerning the Increase of Mankind, Peopling of Countries, Etc.*, Philadelphia, 1751.

6. *An Essay on the Principle of Population*, London, 1798.

renew the basis for his existence through scientific and technological progress.

LaRouche has presented the relationship between relative potential population density and specifically, the energy-flux density used in production processes. There one can see clearly that since the time when men were mere hunters and gatherers, and the energy-flux density of his technologies was extremely low (sun and wind energy), man has been able to increase in numbers by many orders of magnitude due to the increase in energy-flux density, and has a much better living standard, a higher life expectancy, and all told, more human potential. And the next step is already within reach, because China has taken the lead in developing the EAST Fusion program, and has the idea of very soon mining the Moon for helium-3 as a raw material for the coming fusion economy on Earth.

A scene from the silent German film Frau im Mond *(Woman in the Moon) which premiered Oct. 15, 1929 at the UFA-Palast am Zoo cinema in Berlin.*

Ehricke and the Next Stage in Evolution

What does all this have to do with Krafft Ehricke? Ehricke stated very clearly that the opening up of space and its colonization are the necessary next steps in the evolution of mankind. He developed in a wonderful way how life went from the oceans to the continents with the help of photosynthesis, which he described interestingly as the "first industrial revolution," which overcame the "limits to growth" of the time. He described how creatures which were higher on the evolutionary scale, whose metabolisms had a higher energy-flux density, developed until finally man appeared.

And man is absolutely different from all previous forms of life because, according to Ehricke, he has something that he calls "information metabolism"—the ability to absorb information, to differentiate different aspects of it through abstraction, then accumulate it and make use of it both with mind and with machines.

He emphasizes that animals are doubtless intelligent, that they can even learn incredible things, such as how to manipulate human beings, which requires a high level of intelligence. But no animal is capable of abstraction, while man can overcome any limitation. His three fundamental laws of astronautics were already mentioned this morning: The first law is that, under the natural law of this universe, nothing and no one imposes any restrictions on man, except man himself.

This is very, very important, for this is the image of man that was once the norm in Europe. This is identical with humanism, with the Classical idea, which is in turn identical with Platonic philosophy and Christianity, which regards man as a boundlessly perfectible being, both with regard to his mental faculties and his character, and with regard to his emotions and his aesthetic development, there are just as few bounds. This was the normal image of Man, and if you read, for example, Plato, Augustine, Nicholas of Cusa, Leibniz, or Kepler, then you will find precisely this image.

Today, unfortunately, it is no longer self-evident, but Krafft Ehricke said that the human mind can ceaselessly metabolize information "from the infinitesimal to the infinite and, on the infrastructure of knowledge, pursues its moral and social aspirations for a larger and better world against many odds. Through intelligences like ourselves, the universe, and we in it, move into the focus of self-recognition; metal ore is turned into information processing computers, satellites and deep-space probes; and atoms are fused as in stars." And then he says, "I cannot imagine a more foreboding, apocalyptic vision of the future than a mankind endowed with cosmic powers but condemned to solitary confinement on one small planet." That is very true.

Krafft was inspired as a twelve-year-old boy when he saw Fritz Lang's film, *The Woman on the Moon*. He also enormously inspired my husband, who then made another documentary, *The Woman on Mars*. It was this idea that man can leave the Earth's surface, travel in space, and settle other heavenly bodies that fascinated him.

It has already been mentioned that he was present in

Peenemünde—he was just 25 years old—when the first rocket successfully lifted off from Earth on October 3, 1942, and went into space. He was only a hundred yards away, watching the countdown, the ignition, and then the giant roar as the rocket achieved liftoff. And he said, "This was an indescribable feeling, which we all had, we were absolutely conscious that this was the beginning of a new epoch, the first day of the Space Age, the beginning of a completely new era."

Krafft Ehricke defined the "extraterrestrial imperative" as the true identity of humanity. He said that the colonization of the Moon is the obvious first step because it is very close, it takes only two or three days to get there, and now it's even less, and we can essentially practice on the Moon what we will later do on other planets. And what we can do on the Moon, we can do everywhere.

He thought that the colonization of the Moon would take the reverse direction to the evolution on Earth, where the biosphere first developed and then, in a late phase, man had emerged, while on the Moon it would be the other way round: The arrival of man, and then the conditions for his existence. In the first phase, man would bring materials from Earth to the Moon; the second phase would involve the industrialization of the Moon using available resources; and the third would be interplanetary journeys from which new human civilizations would emerge, with completely different characteristics than civilization on Earth.

And he then gave an example of his own "extra-europeanization," as he called it, to illustrate this difference. He said he grew up in Germany, and received a wonderful Classical education. European culture was what shaped him, and when he then emigrated to the United States with his wife, he met a completely different sort of people there, Americans. His children were quite well Americanized, but still had characteristics of the culture of their parents from Germany, whereas his grandchildren were so Americanized that no difference could be discerned.

And he says the same thing will happen in future civilizations in space: The population on the Moon will have completely different physiological and immunological characteristics than the people on Earth.

The New Paradigm

What is being presented here is really the new paradigm that comes from the continuous development of the human species. Chinese President Xi Jinping has often described it as a "community of destiny for the future of mankind," in which the common goals of mankind come first, and the interests of the individual nations come second.

This is precisely the principle of "win-win cooperation," a confluence of different corridors that benefit from improvements in all of the participating countries because it makes no sense to build a railway from one city to another, and then stop, but rather these systems should be integrated to the advantage of all. China's State Councilor Yang Jiechi recently said at the National People's Congress in Beijing that the New Silk Road is not a solo for China, but rather a symphony in which all the peoples and nations participate.

I am absolutely convinced of this, perhaps because I have the advantage of having been in China for the first time in 1971, in the midst of the horrific Cultural Revolution that made people very unhappy. Compared to that, one can see the enormous development that China has made over the last 40 years, or especially the last 30 years, in which it has replicated a development that took 200 years in the other industrial nations. And this Chinese model of economy is so successful that it is now offered as the New Silk Road for all other states to replicate. Thus we have, for the first time, a chance to overcome poverty and all limitations.

All this is based on the ideas of Confucius. I am truly convinced that China is 95% Confucian, and perhaps 5% Marxist or Communist—the essence of China, the Chinese system, is Confucian thought. This includes, for example, lifelong self-improvement, lifelong learning—that every human being should strive to be a "Zhìzhe," a wise person, and the wise should also define the governing process. Harmony should take place in the development of all, in the family, in the state, and among states.

These are ideas that are not only Chinese, but which also belong to the best European tradition, for example, to Nicholas of Cusa, the founder of modern natural sciences in the fifteenth century, who had the idea that harmony in the macrocosm can only exist when all microcosms develop harmoniously, and every microcosm sees it as its own advantage to promote the other microcosms in the best possible way.

And that is the concept. This means that geopolitics can be overcome by putting the development of all on the agenda. I am absolutely convinced that if there is a good understanding between Trump and Xi Jinping and Trump and Putin—and that is Trump's stated intention, and this is clearly signaled by the Russian and Chinese sides—then we will really find ourselves in a new phase of the human species and will experience a new era.

The Role of Germany

The question is, What role should Germany play in this process?

Well, those of you who live in Germany know, of course, that this is not the dominant way of thinking here. But I think that the New Silk Road has such leverage that either Germany will have second thoughts and jump on board, or Germany and the Europeans will become completely irrelevant.

And this is what the Africans already say: "The Chinese, the Indians, the Japanese are all investing in Africa, while Europe comes and preaches about democracy and human rights, but they are not investing in these projects."

Perhaps I should bring up this picture [**Figure 10**] once again: The refugee crisis should be the moral driver for us to adhere to this development perspective. It is only if we develop Africa—together with Russia, China, India, and other countries, hopefully with the United States—and only if we develop the Middle East and Southwest Asia economically, in the context of the New Silk Road, that we can hope to find a humane solution to the refugee crisis and certainly not by internment camps in Turkey or Egypt or Tunisia, as Mrs. Merkel is attempting to do.

The question is also: Will Mrs. Merkel really be the leader of the "free West" because Trump is now President of the United States? Will she continue the confrontation with Russia if Trump seeks reconciliation? Will she continue to push the confrontation to the borders of Russia? Will she continue to participate in interventionist wars to "save democracy"? No one believes us anyway. The countries of Asia and Africa have long since ceased to believe that Europe or the EU are an appropriate model for democracy or human rights.

Or can we not hope that Germany will play a positive role in the expansion of the New Silk Road? I think that Krafft Ehricke—the image of Man and the vision of the future which he represents—should be the best example for the future of Germany. For Germans were once a people of poets, thinkers, and inventors. And all the many positive contributions made by these many, many great thinkers have irrigated the German economy, the middle class, our standard of living, and cul-

FIGURE 10

Federal Ministry for Europe, Integration and Foreign Affairs
Refugees are turned back at the Greek-Macedonian border.

ture. And it was this culture that brought forth Krafft Ehricke.

Why should not it be possible to revive these ideas?—the ideas of Nicholas of Cusa, Kepler, Leibniz, Gauss, Riemann, Bach, Beethoven, Schubert, Schumann, Brahms, Lessing, Mendelssohn, Schiller, the Humboldts, and the classical culture that Krafft Ehricke represented! And not just for Germany, but in a dialogue of cultures, in which the most beautiful formation, the highest form, enters into a dialogue with the others. We heard it this morning, through German classical music, through classical Chinese music, and that too belongs to the new paradigm, that every child will very soon get to know universal history as it has appeared in all its best forms, and then racism and chauvinism and limitations of all kinds will disappear forever.

XI-TRUMP SUMMIT

A Crucial Meeting for the World

by William Jones

April 2—The meeting between U.S. President Donald Trump and Chinese President Xi Jinping will be a watershed moment for the U.S.-China relationship and a critical event that could determine the direction of world history. While *any* meeting between the heads of these two indispensible nations would have global implications, this particular meeting is especially crucial.

CC/Gage Skidmore
President Donald Trump

Xinhua/Wang Ye
China President Xi Jinping

in 2013 now promises to lift millions of people in other Third World countries out of poverty as the result of a policy of infrastructure investment. China has also taken the initiative for the creation of new international banking institutions, like the Asian Infrastructure Investment Bank (AIIB) and the BRICs countries New Development Bank, which are solely geared to realizing that investment.

The newly elected U.S. President has charted a new course for the U.S. economy, rejecting many of the shibolleths of the traditional "free market" ideology, which have proven disastrous over the decades for many countries—including the United States. He is moving toward returning to the "American System" economics of Alexander Hamilton and Henry Clay, which would involve protection for many U.S. industries which have disappeared, thanks to the avarice of our U.S. industrial and financial layers who sought to reap benefit from the labor of underpaid workers in Third World countries, which has left the American workforce and industries in a condition of absolute devastation.

China, which has successfully utilized the "dictates" of the free market system by entering that system as a low-wage producer, has, through a conscientious government policy of systematically investing in science and technology, moved from its original status of being a low-wage manufacturing center to a higher niche of production capability and skill level in the world economy. Through that policy, China has succeeded in developing its economy, becoming the veritable engine of world economic growth, and has raised over 700 million Chinese out of poverty.

China's development of the Belt and Road Initiative

The question facing the two leaders is, *how do these two policies fit together.* China was concerned about some of the statements made by presidential candidate Trump during the presidential campaign, in which he seemed to blame China for the U.S. economic predicament, and also accepted a phone call from the leader of Taiwan. China was also concerned about the appointment of a couple of outright "China-bashers" like Peter Navarro and Robert Lighthizer to the Trump cabinet, in positions affecting international trade.

This created a great deal of trepidation among the Chinese with regard to the upcoming policies of the new President. Much of this trepidation has since been alleviated by the phone call between President Trump and President Xi in February, in which President Trump reiterated support for the One China policy, that is, recognizing the People's Republic of China as the sole representative of the Chinese people, and expressed a willingness to establish a good working relationship with China on all levels.

More recently, President Trump sent his Secretary of State, Rex Tillerson, to China to meet with his counterparts. There Tillerson surprised his Chinese hosts by using the exact terms that China has insisted must characterize the U.S.-China relationship, namely that it be a relationship with "no conflict, no confrontation, mutual respect and win-win cooperation." Until Tillerson's statement, no U.S. official has ever uttered these words to Chinese leaders.

The fact that the two leaders mutually decided to hold such a summit at a very early stage in the new administration indicates that they both realized that having a mutual understanding of each other's goals and intentions was absolutely crucial and both were obviously confident that such a meeting would be successful.

It is perhaps too soon to expect any resolution of the key issues on which the two sides have differing views, whether it be on the issue of trade policy, or the North Korea nuclear program, which has become the pretext for the United States to place THAAD missiles in South Korea, which China views as a threat to them as well, or the South China Sea, where Chinese territorial claims have received push-back from the United States. Given the fact that the new Administration does not even have all of its cabinet appointees in place in order to review and come up with policy recommendations in these matters, there will probably be no definitive resolution on these matters. These will, of course, be on the agenda of discussion, discussions which President Trump has characterized as difficult.

Will Xi and Trump Work Together on U.S. Infrastructure?

But what can be accomplished in the meeting, which is so crucial to the resolution of any of these issues, is a greater understanding of each other's positions and outlooks. President Trump has often shown himself to be a gracious host in these circumstances, and holding the meeting at one of his homes in Mar-a-Lago, Florida, away from the craziness of the nation's capital, would also be conducive to a more personal and intimate discussion. And when met with the appropriate respect due to a Chinese leader, President Xi often shows a great deal of magnanimity in dealing with foreign leaders, even with those with which he is not totally in agreement.

It is also not entirely out of the question that the two leaders, with very different personalities, might even develop a warm relationship. One cannot also exclude the possibility of some surprises coming out of the encounter which might point the way out of some of the problem areas. While President Trump, who has made it one of the hallmarks of his Administration to make changes in trade policy which would benefit U.S. industry, will make greater use of tariffs and taxes in order to keep some production in the United States and to attract other production. This could possibly have an effect on some Chinese export products to the United States.

But if such a policy were not solely directed toward Chinese products, and is not of such a draconian nature as some of the Chinese "hawks" in the Administration may want to impose, this could be acceptable to China if they received something in return. If China were allowed to buy more U.S. high-tech products, this would also go a long way to eliminate the trade deficit with China.

China also invests heavily in the United States, and President Trump has called for a one trillion dollar investment in the failing U.S. infrastructure. China is presently the greatest producer of infrastructure in the world. In addition, they have expressed, in official statements and in numerous articles, their interest in investing in U.S. infrastructure.

While direct Chinese ownership of strategic infrastructure like railroads or telecommunications might be frowned upon, less strategic areas might be opened up for Chinese investment. Creating a national infrastructure fund or bank in which China could invest at an equal or higher rate of return than they are getting from their extensive holdings of Treasury bills, might also be a means of helping President Trump in realizing his infrastructure promise.

If this were combined with the implementation of Glass-Steagall legislation, this Chinese investment would also provide the basis for stabilizing the U.S. banking system, and it also could reorient to the longer term investment in the U.S. infrastructure program.

A closer relationship between the United States and China, particularly on these economic issues, would go a long way in helping them deal with the other issues that are on the table. U.S.-China cooperation would also help solidify the gains made by China's Belt and Road Initiative. A U.S. development program, especially in the realm of high-speed rail, could turn the New Silk Road project of China into a veritable World Landbridge, as has been proposed by Lyndon and Helga LaRouche. Both President Trump and President Xi are leaders who are clearly focused on the need for increased economic development based on the expansion of infrastructure, and this is what could unite them policy-wise. The United States should accept President Xi's invitation to join the Belt and Road Initiative. If the two leaders can find the wisdom to work together on this issue, then the "American Dream" will converge with the "Chinese Dream" and will create a new paradigm of global development for the entire world.

II. The Naysayers

War Party Leads Anti-Trump Drive

by Robert Ingraham

April 2—The paramount issue of our time is one of War or Peace. For sixteen years, under the regimes of George W. Bush and Barack Obama, the United States has been at war—ongoing colonial war, including regime change, color revolutions, mass drone killings, and assassinations; and then, increasingly under Obama, we witnessed a dramatic escalation toward a strategic military confrontation with both Russia and China.

At the time of his 90th birthday celebration, Lyndon LaRouche forcefully made the argument that the Republican/Democratic two-party system in the United States is dead. Such is the case. What we have today is two different political groupings: a War Party and a Peace Party. Hillary Clinton, Barack Obama, George W. Bush, Dick Cheney, John McCain, and George Soros belong to the former. It is the election of Donald Trump which has reinvigorated the latter.

Donald Trump is not a "Republican President." He campaigned as an individual. He challenged sixteen other candidates in the Republican primaries, almost all of whom were tied to the previous Bush Administration. In the general election, he ran not only against

Hillary Clinton, but against the entrenched pro-war faction within the Republican Party itself. He ran against the eight year record of Barack Obama, but he also ran against the policies and outlook of the Bush/Cheney regime.

If one looks at the unholy alliance that today is seeking to topple the Trump Administration, it includes FBI Director James Comey, former CIA Director John Brennan, and other dirty elements within the covert intelligence community; it includes Democratic Party bagman George Soros and leading Congressional Democrats such as Sen. Charles Schumer; it includes former Vice-President Dick Cheney, Republican Senators John McCain and Lindsey Graham, and other neo-con riffraff remnants from the Bush Administration. What all of these institutions and individuals have in common is their hysterical commitment to get the United States back on track for a military build-up against Russia and China.

At first glance, it seems self-evident that the core of the "get-Trump" apparatus is the right-wing "neo-conservative" crowd, or perhaps—as they are often re-

United States Congress
John McCain

Karen Ballard/White House
Dick Cheney

US Senate
Charles Schumer

Flickr/George Soros-World Economic Forum Annual Meeting Davos 2010
George Soros

White House/Pete Souza

John Brennan (right), then head of Homeland Security, briefing Barack Obama on May 1, 2009.

I. John F. Kennedy— American University, June 10, 1963

Printed below are excerpts from President John Fitzgerald Kennedy's speech at American University, perhaps his greatest speech. A number of astute historians have opined that it was the content of this speech that sealed Kennedy's fate, that placed him in the cross-hairs of the assassin's rifle. For Americans today the question to be asked is, "Do you still believe in the vision outlined by that martyred President?" Hillary Clinton certainly doesn't. The FBI doesn't. Dick Cheney doesn't. Barack Obama doesn't. George Soros doesn't. This is what is at stake in the get-Trump conspiracy.

ferred to today—the "Deep State" phenomenon. Such a characterization, however, although accurate up to a point, is ultimately superficial, in the sense that it does not go to the inner nature of the organized evil that has dominated our national institutions increasingly since the murder of President Kennedy, and most specifically since the attack of September 11, 2001.

The actual nature of the beast that now threatens both constitutional government in the United States as well as world peace, is precisely defined by Barbara Boyd in her historic article "The Insurrection Against the President, And Its British Controllers— Or, Who Really Is George Soros, Anyway?", which appeared in the March 31 issue of *Executive Intelligence Review*. In that article, breathtaking in scope, Mrs. Boyd demonstrates that what we are really battling is the modern British Empire, an empire whose most precious geopolitical interests are threatened by the un-controlled independence of President Donald Trump, and by the initiatives already taken by the President to normalize relations with both Russia and China. It is a matter of great urgency that every literate American study and digest what is contained in that article.

President Kennedy said:

I have, therefore, chosen this time and this place to discuss a topic on which ignorance too often abounds and the truth is too rarely perceived—yet it is the most important topic on earth: world peace.

What kind of peace do I mean? What kind of peace do we seek? Not a Pax Americana enforced on the world by American weapons of war. Not the peace of the grave or the security of the slave. I am talking about genuine peace, the kind of peace that makes life on earth worth living, the kind that enables men and nations to grow and to hope and to build a better life for their children—not merely peace for Americans but peace for all men and women—not merely peace in our time but peace for all time.

I speak of peace, therefore, as the necessary rational end of rational men. I realize that the pursuit of peace is not as dramatic as the pursuit of war—and frequently the words of the pursuer fall on deaf ears. But we have no more urgent task.

Some say that it is useless to speak of world peace or world law or world disarmament—and that it will be useless until the leaders of the Soviet Union adopt a more enlightened attitude. I hope they do. I believe we can help them do it. But I also believe that we must re-examine our own attitude—as individuals and as a Nation—for our attitude is as essential as theirs. And every graduate of this school, every thoughtful citizen who despairs of war and wishes to bring peace, should begin by looking inward—by examining his own attitude toward the possibilities of peace, toward the Soviet Union, toward the course of the Cold War and toward freedom and peace here at home...

First: Let us examine our attitude toward peace itself. Too many of us think it is impossible. Too many think it unreal. But that is a dangerous, defeatist belief. It leads to the conclusion that war is inevitable--that mankind is doomed—that we are gripped by forces we cannot control.

We need not accept that view. Our problems are man-made—therefore, they can be solved by man. And man can be as big as he wants. No problem of human destiny is beyond human beings. Man's reason and spirit have often solved the seemingly unsolvable—and we believe they can do it again.

There is no single, simple key to this peace—no grand or magic formula to be adopted by one or two powers. Genuine peace must be the product of many nations, the sum of many acts. It must be dynamic, not static, changing to meet the challenge of each new generation. For peace is a process—a way of solving problems.

With such a peace, there will still be quarrels and conflicting interests, as there are within families and nations. World peace, like community peace, does not require that each man love his neighbor—it requires only that they live together in mutual tolerance, submitting their disputes to a just and peaceful settlement. And history teaches us that enmities between nations, as between individuals, do not last forever. However fixed our likes and dislikes may seem, the tide of time and events will often bring surprising changes in the relations between nations and neighbors...

Finally, my fellow Americans, let us examine our attitude toward peace and freedom here at home. The quality and spirit of our own society must justify and support our efforts abroad. We must show it in the dedication of our own lives... Wherever we are, we must all, in our daily lives, live up to the age-old faith that peace and freedom walk together. In too many of our cities today, the peace is not secure because the freedom is incomplete.

It is the responsibility of the executive branch at all levels of government—local, State, and National—to provide and protect that freedom for all of our citizens by all means within their authority. It is the responsibility of the legislative branch at all levels, wherever that authority is not now adequate, to make it adequate. And it is the responsibility of all citizens in all sections of this country to respect the rights of all others and to respect the law of the land.

II. When Democrats Once Possessed Moral Courage

There was a time, within the not-too-distant memory of living Americans, when many citizens—including a proud patriotic segment of the "liberal" and "progressive" tendency within the Democratic Party—stood firm against police-state operations hatched and promulgated within the U.S. Intelligence community. There was a time when FBI dirty tricks, NSA surveillance, CIA black-bag operations, and other covert operations were the subject of public outrage, courageous Congressional action and mass protest.

There was a time when President Franklin Roosevelt battled ferociously against Wall Street, and then, after FDR's death, when many of those loyal to him, including Lyndon LaRouche, fought tenaciously against Truman, against the FBI, and against the British efforts to destroy the Roosevelt legacy.

There was a time when hopeful Americans rallied to the vision of peace and international cooperation which President John Kennedy outlined in his American University Speech of 1963. A time when "progressives" yearned for an end to the Cold War conflict with the Soviet Union and China, and the establishment of friendly relations among nations, which might lead to a better future for all.

There was a time when many Americans, including leaders within both of America's two major political parties, recognized that the covert operations of the FBI, CIA, et al., were a direct threat to that vision of peace enunciated by President Kennedy.

There was a time when the FBI targeting of Dr. Martin Luther King became a national scandal. And when J. Edgar Hoover's activities were held up to national contempt.

There was a time when a young Democratic Senator

from Alaska, in 1971, stood up to the 'secret government' and read, on the floor of Congress, from the classified "Pentagon Papers." He then entered 4,100 pages from those Papers into the Congressional Record, so as to reveal the lies that the government was telling the American people.

There was a time, in the 1970s, when a veteran Democratic Congressman from New Jersey likened J. Edgar Hoover to Lavrentiy Beria, the head of the Soviet NKVD, and went toe-to-toe against the FBI, even when it resulted in FBI wiretaps and surveillance and in his eventual frame-up and imprisonment.

Congressional Pictorial Directory

Congressman Cornelius Gallagher, Democrat-New Jersey, compared J. Edgar Hoover to Lavrentiy Beria.

There was a time, in 1975 and 1976, when the Church and Pike Committees launched investigations into the FBI, CIA, NSA and other agencies engaged in covert activity, calling hundreds of witnesses and documenting a plethora of crimes, including blackmail, surveillance, and assassinations.

There was a time, in 1988, when a Democratic Congressman from southern California, the head of the Congressional Black Caucus, charged on the floor of Congress that the FBI had been carrying out a forty year-long targeting of black elected officials, under a policy named *Frühmenschen*. This was partially in response to the FBI opening investigations into more than half of the members of the Congressional Black Caucus.

Such individuals and such actions characterize that which has been best—even heroic—in the living history of the Democratic Party. Will that proud legacy now be for naught?

III. The Intended Coup

On March 30, at a full hearing of the Senate Intelligence Committee, a disreputable batch of "Reds-under-the-beds" spooks were let loose as witnesses in the Senate—and onto the nation's television screens. As the hearing progressed, "Cold War" rhetoric flew through the air. But the terrified, blackmailed Senators were worse lunatics than even their witnesses. The back-and-forth "dialogue" between the anti-Trump witnesses and the terrified Senators might have been scripted by Herbert "I Led Three Lives" Philbrick. The entire hearing could be characterized as American Kabuki Theater, or perhaps more accurately a Minstrel Show, composed of FBI and intelligence community barkers and appropriately servile but deranged and panicked Congressional performers.

As was vividly evident at the hearing, these members of Congress are both terrorized and terrified. The blackmail, surveillance, and even more sinister capabilities of the FBI and other covert agencies have these elected officials scared to death. One eyewitness to the March 30 hearing stated that "the Senators were so wild in their fears, that they often had to be constrained by the witnesses!"

Chaired and co-chaired by Richard Burr (R-NC), and Mark Warner (D-VA), the Senate Committee heard testimony from a number of witnesses, including the dirty spook Roy Godson, a British whore who worked with Ollie North in organizing the Nicaraguan Contras, helped organize the invasion of Iraq, and was a leader of the anti-LaRouche faction within the Reagan Administration. His testimony was riddled with anti-Russian denunciations, whom he kept referring to as "the Soviets." Another witness was Clint Watts, representing FPRI, the so-called Foreign Policy Research Institute of Philadelphia, an ancient, evil red-baiting outfit.

Three days prior to the Senate hearing, former U.S. Vice-President Dick Cheney issued his own personal declaration of war against President Trump. Speaking at a business summit in New Delhi sponsored by the *Economic Times*, Cheney stated that, "There's no question there was a very serious effort made by [Russian President Vladimir] Putin and his government, his organization, to interfere in major ways with our basic fundamental democratic processes. In some quarters, that would be considered an act of war. I think it's a kind of conduct and activity we will see going forward... I would not underestimate the weight that we, as Americans, assign to the Russian attempts to interfere with our internal political processes."

IV. Will Cowardice Lead to War?

To their everlasting shame, many leading Democrats—as well as Republicans—now find themselves in bed with the worst scum of the FBI and the intelligence community. Or, to be even less forgiving, these individuals find themselves in the intimate embrace of the assassins of John F. Kennedy. Do not sympathize with them. They are not the helpless victims of the *Laocoön*; rather, the reality that their choice is self-made only increases the depth of their sin.

Perhaps some Democrats or "liberals" take solace in the anti-Trump role of the "progressive" George Soros as evidence that they are somehow on the side of the angels; but as Barbara Boyd has demonstrated, Soros is nothing but an asset of the British-Deep State faction now pushing for war. The anti-Trump rhetoric which oozes from his orifices is all scripted by the war faction in London. When Dick Cheney and George Soros join hands to bring down a duly elected President, one might hope that this would be sufficient to cause even the most deluded anti-Trump protester to stop and question. The real issue here is not "party politics" but gnawing fear in the hearts of our elected officials.

Rep. Bonnie Watson Coleman (D-N.J.), at a recent hearing of the House Homeland Security Committee, stated, "I think this attack that we've experienced [from Russia] is a form of war, a form of war on our fundamental democratic principles."

Sen. Ben Cardin of Maryland, the ranking Democratic member of that chamber's Foreign Relations Committee, has claimed that the alleged Russian actions amounted to a "political Pearl Harbor."

Rep. Jackie Speier (D-CA) recently stated, "I actually think that their engagement was an act of war, an act of hybrid warfare, and I think that's why the American people should be concerned about it."

Rep. Eric Swalwell (D-CA), has charged, "This past election, our country was attacked. We were attacked by Russia. I see this as an opportunity for everyone on this committee, Republicans and Democrats, to not look in the rear-view window but to look forward and do everything we can to make sure that our country never again allows a foreign adversary to attack us."

This behavior is all fear-driven, within the context of a state apparatus where there are no secrets; where, as Edward Snowden and others have shown, every misdeed, every transgression, of every member of Congress is now an open book to the National Security Agency and their allies. Blackmail, or worse, is the order of the day.

The recent performance of leading Democrats—including Maxine Waters who has already called for President Trump's impeachment—would have all of the farcical makings of an *Opéra bouffe* but for two things. One is that they are all being used: they are the window dressing—albeit a necessary political cover—for the ongoing coup against this President. As such, their cowardice at a time of all out assault on the nation's constitutional government by elements of the "Deep State" amounts to near or actual treason. Second, and of even greater importance, is the determination by elements within the British Empire apparatus to re-start the war drive against Russia and China, an eventuality—were it to be realized—which would render all of these Congressmen as accomplices.

Where is the courage of a Cornelius Gallagher? Where is the courage of a Mike Gravel? Where is the courage of a Hale Boggs? Where is the courage of a Mervyn Dymally? Nowhere to be found in the halls of Congress.

James Comey committed treason on Monday, March 20, when he testified to his participation in a coup against the legitimate government of the United States. The entire investigation on Russia is a fraud. The real crime is the intended coup against a legitimate President of the United States, and the threat to force a world war against Russia and China, which would result in a likely nuclear holocaust. And all of this, simply to mask the dire bankruptcy of the trans-Atlantic financial system and the failed political establishment.

Shall we take up President Kennedy's vision of June, 1963, or shall we succumb to our fears?

The Empire's George Orwell Visits The United States Senate

by Barbara Boyd

April 5—Karl Marx, quoting others before him, famously wrote that when history repeats itself, the first event is tragic, the second a rotten farce. If applied to the March 30 U.S. Senate Intelligence Committee hearing seeking to prove that Russia fixed the 2016 Presidential elections, it would be more precise to say, a rotten, murderous farce.

The Senate hearing was nothing less than a completely British-orchestrated effort to re-ignite the march toward war with Russia by the British Liberal Imperialists (Blimps)—a march interrupted by the defeat of Hillary Clinton and the election of Donald Trump. The hearing's method was a freak show display of 1950s Cold War McCarthyism, with such levels of irrationality, hysteria, and pure incompetence as to subject it to ridicule by anyone with a brain. The terrifying fact is that the Senators involved sat there with perfectly straight faces,discussing how to stop such "attacks" in the future by seriously censoring all U.S. political debate. During this discussion,one of the selected witnesses, Dr. Thomas Rid, actually claimed, seriously, that you know it's not "fake news" manufactured by the clever Russkies *only if it is published in the New York Times or Washington Post.* Small wonder that he hails from the London college which trains the British intelligence services.

The next day, April Fool's Day, the Russians appropriately mocked the proceedings by recording a message for their embassy's call-in lines stating: "You have reached the Russian Embassy, your call is very important to us. To arrange a call from a Russian diplomat to your political opponent, press 1; To use the services of Russian hackers, press 2; To request election interference, press 3."

Award-winning journalist Robert Parry was similarly struck by the absurdity of the four-hour Senate

RUSSIA & 2016 ELECTIONS

Senate Intelligence Committee
Dirksen Office Building

C-SPAN3
c-span.org

C-SPAN

The March 30, 2017 Senate Intelligence Committee hearing.

event. He wrote: "It's almost comical how everything that happens in the United States gets blamed on Russia! Russia! Russia! And if any American points out the absurdity of this argument, he or she must be a 'Moscow stooge' or a 'Putin Puppet.' ... When Hillary Clinton boots a presidential election that was literally hers to lose, you might have thought that she lost because she insisted on channeling her State Department emails through a private server that endangered national security, that she gave paid speeches to Wall Street and then tried to hide the content from voters, that she called half of Donald Trump's supporters 'deplorables,' that she was an establishment candidate in an anti-establishment year. ... As we should all know in our properly restructured memory banks and our rearranged sense of reality, it was all Russia's fault! Russia did it by undermining our democratic process through the clever means of releasing truthful information via *Wikileaks* that provided evidence of how the Democratic National Committee rigged the nomination process against Senator Bernie Sanders, revealed the contents of Clinton's hidden Wall Street speeches, and exposed pay-to-play features of the Clinton Foundation in its dealings with foreign entities."

Parry goes on mocking similar inanities from the hearing itself. But, this farce has deadly potential consequences. In the hearing itself, Senator Mark Warner, in a fit of pique, alluded to recent street demonstrations against corruption in Moscow in such as a way as to invite the conclusion that they were set into motion by the United States in retaliation for the wildly alleged and completely unproven Russian hack. Warner said that Premier Medvedev's computers were hacked, resulting in release of information about his corruption and demonstrations in the streets of Moscow. Warner's disclosures, at the end of the hearing, were in response to veiled criticism by witnesses of tit-for-tat warfare where the United States is the far more vulnerable party. Remember, that Barack Obama warned in December that he was setting into a motion a series of undisclosed retaliatory measures. This week, a suicide bomber killed fourteen people in the St. Petersburg subway and injured many others while President Putin was in the city. As this article goes to press, on April 5, a chemical weapons attack is claimed to have taken place in Syria, and the Assad government is being blamed, along with Barack Obama, by the Trump Administration, at least at this point, for the attack. The attack, in an area controlled by al-Qaeda, followed the announcement on March 31 that the Trump Administration was no longer pursuing the overthrow of Assad.

Helpful Events Outside the Zoo

This anti-Russia Trumpgate insurrection has started to fall apart, as the actual treasonous and unconstitutional conspiracy against Trump—and against the U.S. Constitution—is now beginning to come to light. Here is a counterintelligence reminder: When someone like House Intelligence Committee Chair Devin Nunes is pilloried for weeks by the main street media and bobbleheads like Adam Schiff, it generally means they are holding cards which are very dangerous to the Blimp establishment. In Nunes' case, the cards involve documents and source reports showing that the Obama Administration was spying on candidate Trump and his transition team, as far back as 2015 and leaking classified information to the news media in an effort to seal Trump's electoral defeat, or, following the election, cause his removal from office.

The *Weekly Caller*, relying on multiple sources, said on April 4, that Obama's National Security Advisor Susan Rice had been systematically unmasking names of Trump associates in signals intelligence reports since 2015 and discussing them with a circle of Obama officials including her deputy Ben Rhodes, others on Obama's National Security Council, James Clapper, Obama's Director of National Intelligence, CIA Director John Brennan, and Defense Department officials. Other published and source reports this week put Brennan and Clapper at the center of a surveillance and leak conspiracy aimed initially at defeating Trump and subsequently at ousting him from office by any means necessary.

It now is provable that this chain of events was wholly instigated by British intelligence beginning in 2015, when the Brits became "concerned" about Trump's statements proposing détente with Putin's Russia, and set out to discredit him. That "concern" was shared by their American agents, such as Obama, Susan Rice, Evelyn Farkas, Brennan, etc., but not really acted upon because of the belief that Hillary Clinton would win the election in a cake walk and Trump would discredit himself. When Trump won the election, the present efforts to mount a coup began in earnest.

On March 29, Robert Parry reported that Christopher Steele, the British intelligence author of the "cash for trash" dodgy dossier on Trump began working for Hillary Clinton's campaign in June 2016, but had been hired previously by Trump's Republican opponents, and had been an FBI informant concerning events in Ukraine and Russia from 2013-2016. He also was well-known to the FBI from his work heading the MI6 Russia desk. All of Steele's reports were read by Obama's intelligence team and investigated by them, but they were unable to corroborate the hearsay trash in his reports with actual evidence. Nonetheless they deemed Steele a credible source and Steele's reports were leaked to the news media by the Clinton campaign and others, coincident with his debriefing by the FBI in October 2016. According to the BBC, Steele believed that his reports "could swing the election."

The investigation of Steele's utterly bogus claims produced multiple levels of surveillance under E.O. 12333, FISA, and by Britain's GCHQ, of Trump and his associates from the instigation of the investigation forward. These efforts were stepped up when Trump won the Republican nomination, hence the dating of Comey's FBI investigation from July 2016 forward. It is the oldest trick in the Anglo-American intelligence playbook—produce salacious and fabricated claims against a target to create an investigation, use whatever dirt you can find, and use the news media to produce a popular conviction without trial while boxing the target into a pacified, "neutralized" position.

According to Parry, Steele produced 17 reports for Clinton from June 2016 through Dec. 13, 2016 at an estimated cost of over $1,000,000. A deal by the FBI to continue to pay Steele to investigate, reportedly fell apart. The House Intelligence Committee Democrats base all of their claims on Steele's dodgy dossier. The FBI's investigation is based on Steele's reports. It is now also clear that Steele's trash reports are at the heart of the Senate's bizarre March 30 hearing on "Active Measures" and its investigation as well.

Robert Parry reports that Steele's Sept. 14, 2016 report, for example, claimed that Putin devised an active measures campaign to push candidate Clinton away from Obama's trade deals and other Obama policies. In other words, according to Britain's Steele, Bernie Sanders, Elizabeth Warren, and Donald Trump were all tricked by the ever clever Kremlin to oppose controversial trade deals widely opposed by an American public. According to the BBC report, Steele and the Obama Administration concocted the crazed claim that there was a three headed operation by the Russians and Trump.

- First, steal the emails of Democratic Party officials.
- Then push stories based on the hacked information to Twitter and Facebook using bots and the Russian language publications *RT* and *Sputnik*, as well as right wing websites such as *Infowars*, *Breitbart* and *Fox*, from whence the main-stream media becomes an unwitting accomplice.
- Third, use the voter roles for micro-targeting these fake news messages to key contested precincts in swing states, a job which required, according to the Brits and Obama, cooperation by the Trump team. *Voila!* The Russians actually stole the election.

On March 1, 2017, the *New York Times* revealed that Obama and his national security colleagues had spent the months after the election dropping a trail of "leads" in official documents and leaking information, in the effort to destroy Trump and to continue their policies against Russia and China. Elizabeth Farkas confirmed this in an interview with MSNBC on March 3. She was the most senior authority on Russia at the Defense Department and left the Obama Administration in 2015 because she wanted to provide lethal weaponry to Ukraine, and Obama would not do so. She became a key advisor on Russia to Hillary Clinton and is now at the NATO megaphone called the Atlantic Council, which also features CrowdStrike's Dmitri Alperovitch.

According to a March 31, 2017, NBC News report, the document numbers of classified documents resulting from Obama's espionage campaign against Trump were hand-carried by Obama's people to none other than the Senate Intelligence Committee in order to fuel their investigation. And Devin Nunes did what, now? Met with a source in the Executive Office Building due to security concerns? The hubris of Obama's people is truly amazing.

Thankfully, at least some on the House Intelligence side are on the right track and probably now hold the keys to turning the investigation on its appropriate targets, including, specifically, the British. On the Senate side, Senator Grassley, whose Judiciary Committee has jurisdiction over the FBI, is also demanding answers about the relationships between the FBI, Christopher Steele, and the Clinton campaign, citing the unprecedented and illegal nature of the witchhunt against Trump. The House Committee and the Senate Judiciary Committee must also take into account the latest re-

Select Committee on Intelligence

Senator Richard Burr at a Senate Intelligence Committee hearing, March 30, 2017.

Select Committee on Intelligence

Senator Mark Warner questioning a witness at a Senate Intelligence Committee hearing, March 30, 2017.

Select Committee on Intelligence

Dr. Roy Godson testifying on alleged Russian active measures and campaigns of influence, March 30, 2017.

lease from *Wikileaks* demonstrating that the CIA and its Five Eyes partners all have the ability to hack political targets and to disguise these attacks as coming from other state actors, such as Russia. This produces yet further evidence that no Russian hack of the DNC or Podesta in fact occurred, let alone that the products of the hack were shared with *Wikileaks*—creating a complete hole in the "Russia did it" scenario which even Barack Obama has acknowledged.

Inside the Senate Event Itself—Spacebugs?

To understand how something as bizarre as the March 30 event could occur, you have to know something about the Senate Intelligence Committee itself. This is a Committee which has never really challenged the burgeoning police state which arose in the wake of 9/11. The one substantial challenge it made, in its report of CIA torture and other crimes committed in the Bush Administration, was sabotaged by CIA officials, led by John Brennan, using tactics which should have landed Brennan and friends in jail. Long story short: the CIA hacked the Senate investigators' computers, an outrageous and illegal act, and Barack Obama backed Brennan up, and tried to suppress the Committee's entire report. Diane Feinstein, standing alone on the Senate floor and arguing for a severely redacted version of the facts because she had to launch a rear guard defense of her staffers while maintaining her own "credibility" with her colleagues, tells you everything about who is in charge here.

The current leadership of the Committee is com-

posed of Senator Mark Warner, a stooge for Wall Street with pretenses, and Richard Burr, a former appliance salesman from North Carolina who probably got hit in the head too many times playing football. Warner and Burr are involved in a "bromance" which consists of them appearing frequently in front of television cameras to fawn all over one another, declare how much they trust each other, and solemnly pronounce that they will go "where the facts" lead. Hardly a daring intellectual endeavor since they have already been fed all of the "facts" they are to produce.

The first hearing in the morning consisted of Roy Godson of Georgetown University and the Foreign Policy Research Institute of Robert Strausz-Hupé, and Clinton Watts, a former FBI Agent also associated with FRPI and the George Washington University's Center for Cyber and Homeland Security. The third morning panelist was Dr. Eugene Rumer of the Carnegie Endowment and Obama's National Intelligence chair for Russia and Eurasia. You know you have entered the twilight zone when Obama's guy actually appears to be the only sane person in the room.

We can provide detailed testimony showing that Godson is an Anglo-American practitioner of the very black arts that he ascribes to the Russians, and which are now being employed against Donald Trump. In the 1970s, Godson, who was well known to the FBI as a British intelligence/CIA pedigreed snot, went to the FBI with a fabricated report that Lyndon LaRouche was a Russian agent about to engage in terroristic violence throughout the United States. He was joined by Tom

C-SPAN

RUSSIA & 2016 ELECTIONS
CLINTON WATTS
George Washington Center for Cyber &
Homeland Security - Senior Fellow

Clinton Watts testifying at the March 30, 2017 Senate Intelligence Committee hearing.

Kahn, head of the AFL-CIOs international department, which was the home of the CIA's Jay Lovestone, Irving Brown, and Godson's father, Joseph Godson who worked for NATO and the CIA out of the U.S. Embassy in London. These bogus allegations led to a full-scale continuing FBI investigation of LaRouche and his associates.

When that investigation ended because there was absolutely no evidence to support it, Godson played a key role slandering LaRouche inside the Reagan Administration after LaRouche collaborated with President Reagan on the Strategic Defense Initiative (SDI). He went on to participate in planning the propaganda assault against LaRouche during meetings run by George H.W. Bush's CIA and CCF crony, John Train at Freedom House during 1983-84. These meetings involved a huge network of journalists who ran the coordinated media defamations that set the climate for La-Rouche's bogus federal prosecutions.

We are not the only ones who believe Godson is a lying overrated scumbag. Iran/Contra Special Counsel Lawrence Walsh nailed Godson as a key person in Ollie North's Iran/Contra money-laundering schemes to the drug trafficking Contras. Walsh alleged that Godson employed the Heritage Foundation for this purpose. You would have thought that Walsh's Report would have disqualified Godson as an expert witness to anything, but, after all, this is Washington.

At any rate, Roy gave a wandering and rambling presentation about how the Soviets (he couldn't really get himself out of the Cold War in his testimony and kept correcting his repeated use of the Soviet Union to, er, Russia) have historically used propaganda to "punch above their weight." He claimed that the Soviets or Russians have continuously employed 10,000 to 15,000 people burrowing into the minds of the American public with the idea of actually dictating public opinion on essential issues. While there was a slight lull in this ceaseless activity during the 1990s (when Russia, was, of course, flat on its back and being mercilessly looted by the West), it went back to full throttle under Putin. When asked about what countermeasures might be taken, he lauded his work in black propaganda operations under NSDD 77 during the Reagan Administration and the National Endowment (NED) for Democracy, the agency he helped create during the Reagan Administration which has supplemented the CIA in overthrowing democratically elected governments throughout the world. Godson is a frequent collaborator with the NED apparatus currently.

Godson was overshadowed, however, by the insane presentation made by Clint Watts—a true reds-under-every-bed freak show. Watts looks and acts like Don Knotts playing Barney Fife, with the addition of some sort of steroid. He implied that Marco Rubio's defeat in the election somehow was the product of Russian election hacking and that current attacks on Paul Ryan's absolute incompetence in the healthcare debacle were also a Russian active measures feat. Disregard the fact that Rubio was a completely flawed candidate whose robotic repetition of his script during the debates effectively destroyed his candidacy on national television, or that everyone in America hated Ryan's bill. He also said that Donald Trump was an unwitting or witting Russian tool and that he was in fear of his life because the United States did not have an adversarial posture toward Russia. Watts' testimony was largely a repeat of his *War on the Rocks* article called, "Trolling for Trump: How Russia is Trying to Destroy our Democracy." If you want to explore his craziness further you can read it there. Echoing Christopher Steele, both Godson and Watts claimed that the Russian Active Measures campaign involving Trump actually began in 2009 and was carried forward into 2016.

The fake methodology being employed was obvious from the opening of the panel. The methodology assumes that grievances in the United States only exist because of Putin's propaganda techniques. The methodology admits that United States has genuine social problems: it has the problem of race, it has the problem of a depressed economy, it has the problem of massive drug use and suicide, it has the problem of endlessly engaging in genocidal wars for British geopolitical purposes and lying to its population about sacrificing its young in these endeavors. The best propaganda involves elements of truth. Hence, the fact that a normally passive and confused population actually cared about these issues in the last election must be a Soviet plot.

The panel's afternoon session began with a reading by Mark Warner of the three-headed-monster scenario about fake news put forward by Christopher Steele and the Obama Administration. Warner's entire thesis was almost immediately disproved by Colonel Pat Lang in an article at *Sic Semper Tyrannis* published that day, March 30. Warner claimed that if you googled election hacking in the period leading up to the election you would get four or five stories that were Russian propaganda rather than reliable news sources. Pat Lang googled election hacking during that period as Warner suggested and found stories from *Politico*, *Esquire*, *USA Today*, *Bloomberg*, and *CNN*, and not a single Russian source. Warner claimed that stories about the DNC hacks and the Podesta hacks dominated Clinton's news coverage. Again, the evidence shows that the contents of the hacks were almost entirely ignored by the mainstream media who attacked Trump mercilessly while praising Clinton, with only an occasional focus on Clinton's email scandal. Lang concludes: "The claim that Russian propaganda entities—RT and *Sputnik News,* along with paid internet trolls—undermined Hillary Clinton ... requires you suspend all intelligent thought, develop Alzheimer's disease, and refuse to look at any facts. Ignore the fact that Hillary Clinton did not spend much time or money in places like Michigan, Wisconsin, and Pennsylvania. Ignore the dissembling that Hillary engaged in . . . Ignore her shrill voice and robotic appearance. Ignore her passing out on 11 September 2016. Ignore all this and just blame the Russians for the Democratic debacle."

The afternoon session otherwise featured Dr. Thomas Rid of the War Studies Department, King's College London. The Department brags on its website that it is a truly unique institution in the world featuring established relations with British institutions like Chatham House and IISS—and Whitehall being only a five minute walk away. It also featured Keith Alexander, the former head of the NSA, who attacked Edward Snowden as a Russian agent, and Kevin Mandia of the cybersecurity firm FireEye.

The panel completely dispensed early on with any serious inquiry into facts by asking each one of these witnesses whether they believed that Russia was involved in an attempt to influence the 2016 elections—garnering the simple response, "yes," without much further ado. The Russian objectives in this campaign, according to the panel, were to drive wedges between and within U.S. political parties, drive wedges between the United States and NATO, destroy the European Union, and within NATO, to drive wedges between various countries, including influencing upcoming elections in France and Germany. Again, this conclusion ignores the very real economic depression afflicting the West and assumes real grievances only persist because of Putin's propaganda techniques.

Dr. Rid echoed Clint Watts wildman role from the morning, claiming that between March 2015 and May 2016 the Russkies targeted more than 2,000 individuals, including the full-time staff of the Clinton campaign, and that the Russians used *Wikileaks*, *Twitter*, and overeager journalists compelled by the demands of the news cycle, to spread propaganda against Hillary Clinton. He more or less demanded that *RT's* license to operate in the United States be pulled and stated that the only true news in the United States was in the *New York Times* and *Washington Post*.

Alexander and Rid then engaged in a series of exchanges with the Senators regarding what to do about this. According to both, private internet companies must fully cooperate with the U.S. government in anti-Russian cyberops, fully integrating with the NSA, FBI, and like agencies. In essence, in soothing tones, the panelists are proposing a full-scale Orwellian surveillance state, even worse than our compromised semi-Constitutional state of today. As Senator Susan Collins pointed out, the framework for this is already provided in Section 501 of the Intelligence Authorization Bill for 2017, setting up a private/public partnership committee to counter Russian Active Measures (none of which, of course, have really even been proven).

JASON ROSS AND RAY MCGOVERN

The Deep State Behind Trumpgate

The following is selected and edited from the LaRouche PAC Weekly Webcast of March 31, 2017, and includes comments by Jason Ross and transcripts of two film clips from an interview *with Ray McGovern, the co-founder of Veteran Intelligence Professionals for Sanity.*

Jason Ross: The first aspect we're going to be dealing with is what's called "Trumpgate," or the idea that Vladimir Putin not only put Trump in power, but is actually running the Trump administration and setting policy. To discuss that with us, we had an interview earlier today with retired CIA analyst Ray McGovern; who worked in the CIA for decades and is one of the co-founders of VIPS, Veteran Intelligence Professionals for Sanity ...

FIRST VIDEO CLIP:

Ross: Ever since Trump was elected, and especially since his inauguration, there has been a growing chorus of claims about Vladimir Putin putting Trump in office by directing the election, and of even directing Trump's policy. That, in effect, Vladimir Putin is running the United States government. So, is this true?

Ray McGovern: Well, if it is, then I don't know anything about Russia or the Soviet Union. I was counting up the years that I've been immersed in Russian studies; it goes back 59 years when I decided to major in Russian, got my graduate degree in Russian. Taught Russian; was the head of the Soviet foreign policy branch at the CIA; briefed Presidents on Gorbachov. I like to think I learned something about how Russian leaders look at the world.

When I heard this meme going around that Vladimir Putin clearly preferred Donald Trump, my notion was, well, here's Vladimir Putin sitting with his advisors, and he's saying, "That Trump fellow—he's not only unpredictable, but he's proud of it. He brags about it, and he lashes out strongly at every slight, whether it's real or imagined. This is just the guy I want to have his finger on the nuclear codes across the ocean." It boggles the mind that Vladimir Putin would have had any preference for Donald Trump. That's aside from the fact that everyone—and that would include Vladimir Putin, unless he's clairvoyant—knew that Hillary was going to win.

So, just to pursue this thing very briefly, if the major premise is that Vladimir Putin and the terrible Russians wanted Trump to win, then you have a syllogism. Therefore, they tried to help him; therefore, they did all kinds of things to help him. But if you don't accept that major premise, the whole syllogism falls apart, and I don't accept that major premise. Putin said it himself: "I don't have a preference." And I didn't have any preference; I happened to be in Germany during the election, in Berlin. It was exciting, because the German anchors didn't know what to say, to make of it; and my German friends were saying, "We have a German expression here: The choice

Ray McGovern

EIRNS

between Trump and Hillary Clinton is *eine Wahl zwischen Pest und Cholera.*" That means it's a choice between plague and cholera. I said, "You know, I kind of agree."

That's the way I looked at it. I kind of think that's the way Putin looked at it, and when he said, "I don't have any preference," he probably meant he didn't have any preference. So, that syllogism falls down.

Now, just pursue that one little bit here. Everyone expected Hillary to win; everyone. We're talking summer; we're talking fall as Trump disgraced himself in one manner or another. He could never win, right? And nobody thought that Hillary was such a flawed candidate that nobody trusted her, that she might lose. So, you hear what I'm saying? "Well, it looks like Hillary is going to win. Looks pretty sure she's going to win. So, why not hack into her mechanism there in the Democratic National Committee? If I get caught, well she may be angry with me, but what's to lose?" I don't think so. Putin is a very cautious fellow. If he thought Hillary was going to win, like the rest of us did, the last thing he would want to do is hack into their DNC apparatus and be caught; because he would likely be caught. And have an additional grievance for Hillary to advertise against him. So, it falls down on logic alone.

Now, luckily, you mentioned Veteran Intelligence Professionals for Sanity. We are the beneficiary of a membership whose expertise in intelligence matters just won't quit. This includes four former high officials in the National Security Agency—retired; one of whom devised all of these collection systems that NSA is still using. His name is Bill Binney. He and I are very close. He writes for us, and he helps me write things. What he has said from the outset—and this is five months ago—is that this could not be a hack; it had to be a leak. And for your your viewers, a hack goes over the network.

Ross: You're speaking of the DNC?

McGovern: Yeah, I'm talking about the Russians— thanks for interrupting; the Russians are accused, of course, of hacking into the Democratic National Committee emails, and they're also accused of surfacing the Podesta emails. Bill says, "Look, I know this network; I created pretty much the bones of it. And, I'm free to talk about it. Why? Here are the slides that Ed Snowden brought out; here are the trace points, the trace mechanism. And there are hundreds in the network. So, everything that goes across the network, Ray, and I know this is hard for you to believe, and you're looking at me real strange, but *everything*. You know where it starts and you know where it ends up, everything." So, if this was a hack, NSA would know about it. NSA does not know about it.

As a matter of fact, the CIA and the FBI said, "We have high confidence that the Russians did this." But the NSA, which is the only real agency that has the capability to trace this, said "We only have moderate confidence." In the Army, we called that the SWAG

C-SPAN

FBI Director James Comey (center) testifying at a House Select Intelligence Committee hearing on alleged Russian interference in the 2016 U.S. Presidential election.

factor—it's a Scientific Wild-Assed Guess. So NSA doesn't have the information. If they had the information, I'm pretty sure they would release it, because this is not rocket science. Everybody knows how these things work, particularly since Ed Snowden revealed the whole kit and caboodle.

The Surveillance State

Ross: Ray McGovern and Bill Binney co-authored an article three days ago, called "The Surveillance State Behind Russia-gate." I want to read a very short part of it. They write:

Although many details are still hazy because of secrecy—and further befogged by politics—it appears House Intelligence Committee Chairman Devin Nunes was informed last week about invasive electronic surveillance of senior U.S. government officials and, in turn, passed that information on to President Trump.

This news presents Trump with an unwelcome but unavoidable choice: Confront those who have kept him in the dark about such rogue activities or live fearfully in their shadow. ...

What President Trump decides will largely determine the freedom of action he enjoys as President on many key security and other issues. But even more so, his choice may decide whether there is a future for this constitutional republic.

Very strong words. In the past month, on March 4, we saw Trump's announcement that he was surveilled by the outgoing Obama administration; he used the word "wiretap" at times, for which he was attacked for his choice of language. But the statement still stands about surveillance. On March 20, FBI Director Comey testified that he was investigating the Trump administration; guess he didn't have any time to investigate the Saudis.

Just today, Wikileaks came out with a report in which it released the latest section of what they are calling "Vault 7," which is a collection of material from the CIA —documentation and source code. What this latest release showed was "Project Marble," as the CIA called it, which revealed a program that they have to obfuscate their own creation of cyber weaponry, of malware and other types of attacks, and the ability to easily attribute such attacks to other state actors—including the ability to make it look as though an attack came from Russia, also including a seeming cover-up of Russian tracks so that a security researcher might feel that they had stumbled across a clue by finding Russian language comments in this cyber attack weapon, when really it had been planted from the beginning. This of course raises the question of attribution at all, and in particular about the DNC hacks.

The FBI never investigated the DNC computers, and all the complaints about Russian involvement and Russian malware came from CrowdStrike, an independent firm … All signs point to this and the Podesta emails being leaks rather than hacks anyway.

So, let's hear our second clip that we have for the program from our interview with Ray McGovern.

"The CIA has 'six ways to Sunday' to get at you …"

cia.gov

SECOND VIDEO CLIP:

McGovern: I think Nunes wants to do the right thing. Whether he'll succeed or not is anybody's guess. All I can say is, he's up against formidable opponents; witness what the ranking member or minority leader of the Senate, Chuck Schumer, has said outright to Rachel Maddow.

He says, "You know, I thought Trump was a really smart guy. But he's done something very foolish." What's that? "Well, he's taken on the CIA"—now this is Schumer—"and the CIA has six ways from Sunday to get at you. So, whereas I thought Trump was a reason-ably bright guy, a really good businessman, I'm not so sure anymore, because he's done something very foolish." Now, what does Rachel say? Well, if you were Rachel, if I were Rachel, I think I would have said, "Senator Schumer, are you saying that the President of the United States should be afraid of the CIA? Is that what you're saying?" What she did say was, "Oh, I guess we have to go to break now." So, all I'm saying is, there's the minority head of the Senate, and he's saying "Look, you take on the CIA, they've got six ways to Sunday"—that's an old Bronx expression; I come from the Bronx. "Six ways to Sunday" means six days of the week 'til Sunday to get at you.

So, that was part and parcel of all this. They're afraid.

Ross: Yeah. It puts the rank in ranking.
McGovern: Yeah, you got it!

Ross: I think this story or picture that you've painted really gives us something that we need to do, because if this is to be fought out only among institutional layers, it's a tough fight. It's something where, if people are aware, as we're able to make known to the population more generally, that this is a fight—that this isn't about Democrats versus Republicans,—This is really much more about Deep State versus the potential of elected government to determine our course. The threats of say, blackmail via the FBI or other intelligence agencies, the dossiers that no doubt exist on these elected officials—that stands as a threat if people aren't aware of that being the *modus operandi*.

I think people are more familiar with the way the FBI targeted Martin Luther King, urged him on more than one occasion to commit suicide to prevent these kinds of documents from getting out. I think it really means that there's something for all of us to do in terms of making sure that this is known; making sure that the terms of the fight are known, to make it possible to win this one.

McGovern: Exactly, and those were wiretaps, back in the late '50s, early '60s, those were real wiretaps. You're quite right; that was heinous. Now I asked Coleen

Rowley, who is, as I say, [an example of] the expertise we have available to us at Veteran Intelligence Professionals for Sanity that won't quit. Colleen was the counsel of the Minneapolis division of the FBI; she was the one who wrote memos to the Director saying this is how we screwed up on 9/11. She's got guts that won't quit as well. I said, "Colleen, Robert Kennedy—my God! Robert Kennedy, Attorney General, allowing, authorizing the FBI to try to persuade Dr. King to commit suicide? How do you figure that, Colleen?" And she said, "Ray, wiretapping, J. Edgar Hoover. Bobby Kennedy would know that J. Edgar Hoover has lots of information on all those pretty girls that he and Jack used to invite to the White House pool and all of that stuff."

She's *imagining* this; but the reality is, Robert Kennedy would know that J. Edgar Hoover would have lots of material to blackmail not only him, but his big brother.

That's big; and that's why when all this came out in the mid '70s, they created these laws and created these Oversight Committees, which for a while, did their job. Now, they're hopelessly unable, unwilling; they don't want to know this stuff, and they don't know it for that matter. The intelligence officials say, "They don't want to know this, so why should we tell them?"

As for citizens, I would emphasize that this whole business when Edward Snowden came out with his revelations in June of 2013, what happened? People said, "Well isn't this interesting? Everything—they intercept everything! Emails, telephone calls, wow! Luckily, I have nothing to hide." So, we asked someone from the Stasi—Stasi is the old East German secret service; and if people have seen *Die Leben der Anderen*—"Other People's Lives"—an Academy Award film about East Germany and the Stasi. The Stasi was their KGB. You get a picture of what they did. Wolfgang Schmidt—his real name by the way—a Stasi colonel, is interviewed. One of the Americans sits down and asks, "Wolfgang, what do you think about people in America when we say, 'We have nothing to hide'?"

Schmidt says, "This is incredibly naïve. Everyone has something to hide. You don't get to decide what they get on you. The only way to prevent it from being against you, is to prevent it from being collected in the first place." Beautiful, you know? If they collect it, they can use it. They don't read it all; they don't listen to it all. But they put it into these little files—they're not files, but they're …

So, yeah, *all of us.* What Edward Snowden said about "turnkey tyranny." If you have these kinds of private information about *everyone* including the President and Michael Flynn and all his associates, back in October, November, December; well, you have the ability, if not to win the election, then at least to destroy,— or make these folks seem beholden to the *Russians*, of all places, and disarm the attempts that Trump wants to make, vis-à…-vis Russia.

Now, I would have to tell you, that I am against everything Trump stands for, internally. I think he's not only unqualified to be President, but all his instincts are terrible…. [But] he's right about Russia. If he were to say to Vladimir Putin, "Look, I don't think we need to put more troops in the Baltic states or Poland, so why don't I pull out those troops, and you pull out the troops on the other side? It's a deal?" I'm morally certain Putin would say, "It's a deal!" Now, what would that mean? That would mean what Pope Francis, to his credit, called "the blood-drenched arms traders" would lose out, big time. Peace: bad for business. Tension: very good for business. So, there's a lot at stake among very, very powerful people, and if Trump can make this stick—this is not a puny, incidental issue, it's a transcendental one.

I was more afraid that Hillary would bring us to a nuclear confrontation than Trump. I didn't like Trump on the environment, because I have nine grandchildren. So, for me it was a choice between plague and cholera. But here we have a possibility for a new—what the Germans call *Ostpolitik*—a new policy, looking to the East. Take my word for it; I've looked at what the Russians have done. I've looked at the heyday of the relationship of the United States and Russia, which goes back to October of 2013 when Putin pulled Obama's chestnuts out of the fire by persuading the Syrians to destroy, or have destroyed, all their chemical weapons *on U.S. ships*. Okay? Nobody knows about that but the United States.

But the neocons, the people who want to create a *bad* atmosphere in relations between the United States and Russia—they know about it. It only took them six months to mount a coup on Russia's doorstep in Kiev, Ukraine. And that's where all this trouble started: Russians accused of invading Ukraine—not true; of invading Crimea—not true. All that stuff was artificially pumped up; it's just as easily deflated. And Trump, if he's willing to do that, well, that would be a biggie.

Ross: Great! Thanks very much, Ray. Thanks.
McGovern: You're most welcome. Thanks for asking. It's very rare that I get a chance to review what I observe.

III. An Historic Paper by Lyndon LaRouche From Just Twelve Years Ago

AN EMERGENCY RECONSTRUCTION POLICY

Recreate Our Economy!

by Lyndon H. LaRouche, Jr.

April 2, 2005

At this moment the U.S.A. is gripped by the greatest world monetary-financial crisis of more than a century. Although the U.S. economy itself has been in a process of uninterrupted decline for more than three decades, the majority of our citizens have been in a state of denial of this reality of the onrushing disaster, until most recently. Therefore, the illusion still rampant among leading institutions and the population generally, is that the presently onrushing collapse of the U.S. economy itself dates about the time of the 2001 inauguration of President George W. Bush, Jr. Although George W. Bush, Junior's Administration's policies have aggravated the problem in the extreme, there are no solutions for the threatened sudden, and very deep collapse of the economy, which do not depend upon recognizing that those mistakes in policy and popular opinion which have caused this crisis, have been chiefly the policies which have been supported, or tolerated by our government, and by the majority of the nation, until a recent time.

To convince the population to recognize the actual remedies for today's onrushing deep depression, we must identify those causes as the policies which the majority of popular opinion has considered acceptable, or even demanded, for more than a generation. Until popular opinion is willing to take the blame for its own mistakes of no less than three decades, no solution for the presently onrushing breakdown crisis of the world economy would be possible.

Presently, we hear a growing number of proposals for fixing today's dying U.S. economy. These proposals include some useful observations, but all proposals for merely "fixing" this or that problem within the U.S., or European economies piece by piece, will fail, and that immediately, and that in an awful way. Suggestions of that kind will fail, almost inevitably, because of what they do not say: *You can not heal what you have killed; you can not fix what you have already destroyed.*

So, we must replace the present policies of our government, substituting new policies which are consistent in principle with those which gave us the once excellent economy of more than a generation ago: an economy which the U.S. itself has willfully destroyed since the first inauguration of President Richard M. Nixon. We, as a nation, have destroyed our own economy, by adopting and implementing, or merely tolerating policy-changes which experience has now shown to have been lunacy. These are lunacies which have reigned like obsessions, increasingly, over our economy, and over the policy-shaping trends of our government and leading political parties, for about thirty-five years: in other words, since approximately the aftermath of the death of former President Dwight Eisenhower, and the beginning of that Richard M. Nixon Administration which was run and ruined by the likes of George Pratt Shultz and his crony, Henry A. Kissinger.

Therefore, forget about attempting to talk the garbage into reforming itself; remove it. Replace the foolish laws and misguided majority of popular opinion which, over more than thirty years, have combined their efforts to create what has now become today's mortal threat to the existence of our republic.

To begin, today, our economy faces a similar, but far, far more serious problem than that which had been bequeathed to incoming President Franklin Roosevelt

"For most parts of the United States, the great productive economy which we had, still, had thirty-five years ago, is long gone," LaRouche writes. Above: Detroit's famed Ford River Rouge auto production complex, during better times. Right: A closed Ford River Rouge plant in 2003. Where have those skilled and semi-skilled workers gone?

recovery which existed thirty-five years ago, no longer exist to be fixed today.

So, today, we face a new challenge for reconstruction of our presently dying economy. The situation which Franklin Roosevelt addressed with great relative success, was less severe than that which faces us as the ruined state of our national economy today. The underlying principles expressed by Franklin Roosevelt's successes remain the same; but, radically new kinds of problems must be recognized and taken into account in crafting our designs for a general recovery. [*See endnote.*]

During most of the years since the beginning of 1969, we have been told, and told, and told, over three decades, that our economy has been growing, has been more and more prosperous. The evidence today is, that all those official and other published stories of growth and recovery have been lies; we have bigger lies on this account from our government and Federal Reserve System today than ever before.

Look about us, county by county across the U.S.A. Remember the farms, the infrastructure, the industries, the health-care standards, and so forth, which could be found, about thirty years ago, as a per-capita, per-square-kilometer standard of reference in the conditions of each county. Pull out the photographs taken in most of the great wealth-producing counties of the former agro-industrial regions of our nation thirty-odd and more years ago. Then, holding those pictures before your eyes, see the same locations today.

For most parts of the U.S., the great productive economy which we had, still, thirty-five years ago, is long gone, especially since the mania of deregulation and monetarism under 1977-1981 National Security Advisor Zbigniew Brzezinski. [See **Figure 1-12.**] Thus, while half the currently reported financial wealth of the

as the ruinous legacy of the Coolidge and Hoover administrations. Under Roosevelt, reconstruction of what emerged by Spring 1945 as the most powerful economy the world had ever seen, our U.S. economy of Roosevelt's last years, was built by salvaging the foundations of agricultural and industrial power which were temporarily ruined, but still standing in March 1933. The difference today, is that we have spent more than three decades, since the beginning of the Nixon Administration, in uprooting the greatest part of that great agro-industrial power and infrastructure which had been still standing when Nixon entered office. In large part, many of the elements of a potential U.S. economic population is concentrated among what has become increasingly a hopelessly debt-ridden upper twenty percentile of our family households, the conditions of life of the lower eighty percentile has been consistently down, down, down since about 1977. Our industries are gone, or vanishing, and their productive employment with it. Private pensions is a category which has now almost gone out of existence for the lower eighty percentile of our population, while poor foolish, and ever-lying sadist and Federal Reserve System stooge, President Dubya, tries to sell to what he must hope are the dumb suckers, more of that same doomed paper today.

Simply said, the official reports of the progress of the U.S. economy have been faked, that ever more wildly, over the entirety of the recent three or more decades, as under the succession of Federal Reserve Chairmen Paul A. Volcker and Alan Greenspan.

So far, today's strongest popular political reaction to this decades-long pattern of national economic suicide has come to the surface around the fight to defend Social Security and health-care against the rapacity of Augusto Pinochet's former crony George Pratt Shultz, and Shultz's puppets, such as the George W. Bush, Jr. Administration and that pot-bellied relic of the stone age, the California "Governator," Arnold "Conan" Schwarzenegger.

Now, a titanic change is in the making for the very, very near future. The onrushing collapse of the section of the economy typified by the General Motors complex, when combined with the acute over-ripeness for bust-out of the monstrously speculative U.S.A. and United Kingdom mortgage-bubble markets, produces an effect which intersects the biggest international "Ponzi Scheme" in modern world history, the vast bubble in financial speculation conducted by those super-vast, predatory financier interests whose principal investments are now intended to steal control of the future petroleum and other raw-materials supplies of the entire planet. That is the same bubble of giant financial hoaxes being expressed as the soaring prices in the housing and fuel markets of the present moment.

The precondition for preventing the onrushing chain-reaction collapse of the physical economy of the world from occurring, is to recognize that the present world monetary-financial system itself, the IMF system in its present form, is doomed to an early general collapse. That IMF system itself can not be saved; whatever happens to our economy, for better or worse today, the way the U.S. and international economy has devel-oped since the mid-1960s, is something which will never recover, as that form of economy, or anything like it, within several lifetimes yet to come. If we do not replace the present, implicitly bankrupt system and its policies, by a system based on the same principles used to create the national recovery organized under President Franklin Roosevelt's administration, there is no future worth mentioning for your community or your family—during the decades yet to come.

In the meantime, today, George Pratt Shultz's close association with the forces behind the neo-Nazi, death-squad-linked, Augusto Pinochet of the 1970s and 1980s, is an image of the kind of thinking which the accelerating present world financial crisis prompts in circles typified by Shultz still today: replacement, on a global scale, of democratic forms of self-government by dictatorships echoing the Mussolini, Hitler, Franco, and Pinochet models of earlier times.

Those policies of Shultz, et al., policies such as the desperate effort of President George Bush. Jr. to loot Social Security, reflect the same thinking around today's U.S. Federal Reserve System which Bank of England asset Hjalmar Schacht represented in bringing Adolf Hitler into power in 1933 Germany. We are therefore in a race, to return to the kind of policies, under President Franklin Roosevelt, which enabled the U.S. not only to escape the fate of Nazi rule in continental Europe, but to defeat a Nazi power which was on the verge of establishing an empire over the world.

Tough language? Yes; but, among those who know the facts, only wishful dreamers and whimpering cowards would choose any different language than I have employed here.

Using Resources Which No Longer Exist

You will be told by people who have yet to learn their lessons of experience, that there are clearly available resources which could be mobilized to allow us to fix this or that problem without any more radical change in the present economic system than that. Some of those reports may seem to be almost factually true, on condition that you deceive yourself by limiting your attention to some very narrowly defined parts of our overall national economic crisis. But, they are also as misleading as outright lies would be; they are instances of statistical fraud, intended or not, fraud crafted by fallacy of composition.

The problem is, that if we take all of the interdependent problem-areas, such as providing adequate health-care facilities for an emergency, the conflicting de-

The shutdown of the U.S. steel industry is the hallmark of the "globalization" era. Above: The Bethlehem Steel blast furnace at Sparrows Point, near Baltimore, in the 1970s. Bethlehem Steel. Right: The closed Sparrows Point complex in 1983.

EIRNS/Suzanne Klebe.

many Canadians face under that nation's much-praised, present health-care policy. The right to health care may exist on the statute books, by law; but the means to deliver that health-care to all who need it simply do not exist, physically, in all of the most crucial categories. As Queen Marie Antoinette is reported to have said of the poor of that time, "Let them eat cake." The same would have to be said about any similar, legislated, but unfunded "universal health-care plan" coming out of the U.S. Congress today.

What we require, in the area of health care, for example, is a Hill-Burton-law-modelled policy of building up the health-care capacity to levels adequate to provide the care the wishful ideologues in Congress and elsewhere might propose to guarantee. The effective denial of needed health care to returning U.S. military veterans of Iraq, is typical of the fraud rampant under the current Bush Administration. Morally, you can not legislate the existence of a promised delivery of services, if the capacity to deliver those services as promptly as implied do not exist, and if you fail to provide for the creation of the capacity to perform as the law is read as promising. Government must not allow it to be said, that it has promised something, by stated policy, which, by the currently common sophistry of practiced policy, it refuses to provide.

What is presently true of the health-care system which has been savaged by the Nixon Administration's repeal of the Hill-Burton law, is also true in nearly every area of economic concern in the U.S.A. today. We have a prevalent policy which says, liberally, on the one hand, "Promise them anything, but give them Arpège," and, on the other hand, we have the right-wing cannibals of the Congress who would solve that problem with a policy of, "We must stop giving them Arpège."

You can not provide safe water without rebuilding our nation's water-management system up to standards

mands to be made can not be met, simply because many different proposed solutions are relying upon resources for their program which would have to be taken away from the shrinking mass of resources currently existing among each of a dozen or more, worthy but competing areas of national emergency problems. The illusion that we could fix each of our problems without overturning the present system, is what we used to call a "blind men and the elephant" problem, a fallacy of composition; the fellow who proposes to fix the one problem is overlooking a dozen or more equally deadly problems which are each and all counting upon drawing down the same resources which vitally needed solutions in the other areas would require.

For example, as many well-advised people, in or out of government, would warn you, passing a law which guarantees the citizen's right to access to health care, will make him find himself in the kind of disaster which of the pre-Nixon, pre-Brzezinski era. Without a major national infrastructure-rebuilding program, which must be funded largely through long-term government-created credit at permanently low interest-rates, this U.S. economy would never recover from the presently on-rushing catastrophe.

For example, this means vast investments in generation and distribution of power under very high energy-flux densities at the point of generation. This means a shift out of today's lemming-like run into vast over-emphasis on highway transport, back to the technologically modern frontier levels of safe, high-speed transport of passengers and freight by rail and kindred means. This means, a shift out of petroleum-fueled highway vehicles and local energy supplies, into the general use of hydrogen-based fuels, fuels chiefly produced within regions, as byproducts of high-temperature-reactor, re-regulated, state-wide power systems.

This means radical changes in national educational policy, toward emphasis on universal excellence, away from recent trends and national statutes attuned toward President Bush's passion for dumbed-down school systems, systems designed for an educational program which leaves most graduates far behind the curve of both even simple literacy, as also of modern science and technology.

It means that a reborn U.S.A., and Europe, too, must cease to be an unproductive parasite sucking on the globalized produce of the world's desperately poor peoples, and, instead, serve as a fountain of scientific and technological progress which a revival of our once leading cultural development will enable us to deliver to nations which desire fulfillment of their right to access to the same technological progress.

We must adopt, thus, a mission of supplying the stimulus and assistance needed to uplift the general population of this planet from that planet's swamp-like regions of poverty, disease, and ignorance. These are the economically depraved conditions which we, through the policies insisted upon by financially powerful policy-influencing circles of the U.S.A. and Europe, have promoted, and strictly enforced over a period of about a half a century, in regions such as Asia. The U.S. and other influential agencies have demanded, that these Asian nations must abandon crucially essential, large infrastructural and other technological progress for the often virtually slave-labor kinds of employment opportunities which visiting tourists might wish to enjoy at seaside and kindred hotels and entertainment complexes where they are waited upon by the miserably poor.[1]

These and related foundations of general economic recovery are not matters of existing things which need to be fixed. They represent our vital interest in creating what, unfortunately, presently does not exist to be fixed.

1. The Rebirth of the U.S. Economic System

There is no way in which there could be a survival of the U.S. as a republic, under a continuation of President George W. Bush's combination of tax-free rides for the rich, combined with savage budgetary austerity against absolutely necessary programs for U.S. economic survival, and combined with the lunatic utopians' U.S. defense strategies seen as part of Bush's foreign policies and strategies. To bring the U.S. national economy above budgetary breakeven levels, without massive, capital expenditures, would be impossible. The only remedy is to use U.S. government-created long-term credit, a process of credit-creation which will require the immediate introduction of a number of the perfectly feasible measures which the present Bush Administration and Federal Reserve System have forbidden. These indispensable actions, like the recovery measures under President Franklin Roosevelt earlier, go against everything which the Coolidge, Hoover, and Bush Administrations have represented. They go against everything for which the present Federal Reserve System, the present International Monetary Fund, and the present World Bank stand.

Are you going to continue to tolerate those Bush and Federal Reserve dictates, or, do you prefer that our republic shall outlive the presently onrushing, world-wide, general monetary-financial collapse?

Do not waste your own time, or your neighbor's, arguing that there is any way that the U.S. economy can continue to exist under a continuation of presently operating national and international monetary-financial policies. The entire system is now on the brink of a general breakdown crisis from which it could never recover in anything resembling its current form. Time has run out for debating that issue. The greatest world-wide fi-

---

1. The case of two projects for Southeast Asia are relevant, the Kra Canal and the Mekong development program, as is the case of the suppression of Secretary of State William P. Rogers' development program for Southwest Asia.

White House Photo.

President Bush at the U.S. Treasury Agency's Bureau of Public Debt in Parkersubrg, West Virginia, on April 5, in a grandstanding tour for Social Security privatization. The file cabinet holds the $1.7 trillion in Treasury securities that make up the Social Security trust fund. Bush proclaimed that there were no "real assets" there. "There is no trust fund. Just IOUs that I saw firsthand."

nancial crash in modern history is hanging, like rotten-ripe fruit, ready to drop from the tree at any moment, sooner or not much later. Either prepare to make the kind of changes which memory of President Franklin Roosevelt suggests, or be prepared to experience the virtual economic death of our own and many other nations, very soon.

For the moment, at least, you still do have the freedom for making that very specific kind of choice. That is about as much democracy as the inescapable reality of the present situation has not already taken away from you.

Do not blame me for delivering what some of you might regard as an ultimatum. Nature itself is now hastening on the way to deliver that ultimatum to you personally. It is, in fact, what you, by your stubborn negligence, by the way you voted, or the way you did not vote, have finally delivered to your own doorstep. As

might be said of Iraq today, it is President Bush's and your own "Appointment in Samarra." What I propose as an alternative, is the only option left available to those who would prefer to survive. Sometimes, life is like that. Science is always like that. At some points in time, the fate of empires, and of entire nations such as our own, is like that.

I outline the needed remedies for our situation, step by step, as follows. I explain this in a way needed to make the explanation as easily understood as possible without leaving out anything essential.

What We Must Do

The Federal, state, county, and local governments of the territory of the U.S.A. have a vast accumulation of worthy projects in major maintenance and building of basic economic infrastructure. Many among these are authorized for expenditure as soon as funding is brought forward. The implementation of a sizeable portion of these hundreds of billions of dollars' worth of large accumulation of absolutely necessary and worthy public or private U.S. domestic investments in basic economic infrastructure, would be sufficient to bring the current level of net national income far enough above national breakeven-point, to allow us to bring the presently onrushing monetary-financial crisis of the U.S.A. under control.

The biggest physical obstacle to such recovery measures is the shortage of organized skills and sources of supply to fulfil a sufficient number of such assignments to accomplish the immediately intended result. There is the additional problem, that we must choose a combination of such options which do not conflict fatally with one another in their competition for our scarce present resources. For example, a large chunk of these programs involves the participation of the U.S. Corps of Engineers. We have, presently, a generation's worth of waiting work to be done with participation by the Corps, beginning right now, but there are presently limited resources for that effort.

For example, one of the largest components of our national productive capacity, both for the so-called private and public sectors, is concentrated in the machine-tool-centered capacity of our current aerospace and auto industry. At a time when it would be futile to attempt to maintain current levels of sales of new automobiles, we must think in terms of keeping the high-technology aspect of those industries fully operating, by diversifying the work-load to include urgently needed national programs in infrastructure, such as a new, urgently needed, national railway grid for passengers and freight, as a shift from the threatened early physical breakdown caused by post-World War II over-emphasis on highway transportation.

The general objective of initial, stop-gap adjustments of that type, is to concentrate on mobilizing useful programs which are intended to preserve and strengthen the vital high-technology end of our national productive capacity, by mobilizing what are presently threatened with becoming lost productive resources, while we still have the option of keeping those vital capacities alive.

Thus, although the presently skyrocketing petroleum price is not a reflection of current shortages in petroleum supplies, but, rather, a reflection of wild-eyed speculation in monopolistic efforts to buy up the world's future petroleum stocks, we must begin to shift out of excessive dependency on combustion of petroleum products as a source of power for our nation, and the world at large. At the same time, the highway congestion and related logistical problems of our excessively highway-dependent national economy, require a marginally very large and rapid shift into mass-transport of goods and people, and a shift toward regionally produced hydrogen-based fuels to replace today's relative dependency on consumption of petroleum and natural gas as fuels.

There are also other major objectives to be served by such a reform, but what I have just said gives you the gist of the matter.

Similarly, we have a major water-management crisis, requiring immediate restoration of collapsing systems which use waterways and reservoirs for essential purposes of transportation, production, and human consumption.

We need, immediately, large-scale programs of development of basic economic infrastructure which combine the utilization and expansion of cadres of highly skilled operatives and technologies, but which also absorb large numbers of otherwise unemployed semi-skilled and unskilled labor as an integral part of the same programs. The maintenance and expansion of the ranks of the highly skilled production operative, and the upgrading of the unskilled and less skilled through the same programs which are led by the most skilled, strikes the balance needed for large-scale expansion of productive, rather than services employment, on which the initial phase of a recovery-effort must be premised.

Among the most urgent tasks to be taken on right now, is to put together a consolidated list of all of the relevant productive resources available and investments ready to be made. We must now determine how this combination of possibilities could be put together as a general emergency recovery program for the nation as a whole.

To conduct such a program requires a very large amount of long-term credit at basic rates of about 2% simple-interest per annum over periods of about a quarter-century. This requires a return to a fixed-exchange-rate form of international monetary system, otherwise no general recovery would be possible. Lessons learned under President Franklin Roosevelt, from the 1930s recovery-process and the war-time age of the legendary "Rosie the Riveter," come into play in relevant modes of policy-shaping.

There are tricky features to this kind of effort, especially as a matter of the need to coordinate the physical implications of a national effort along those lines. However, the principle of the business is broadly as I have just summarily described it.

1.1 How To Deal With the Monetary Crisis

Now we come to the really sticky part, the part about handling the world's existing financial-monetary system. This brings us to a crucial matter in principles of international and constitutional law.

The world is presently dominated by the floating exchange-rate form of present monetary-financial system, the present International Monetary Fund (IMF) system. This system, is, in fact, presently bankrupt, hopelessly bankrupt in its present form. It is kept alive, in the sense of a life-support system, chiefly, by a skyrocketing mass of sheer financial-derivatives and other fraud, including the forms of Enron-like, or comparable practices addressed by the New York State prosecutors.

Typical of the principal means being used currently to postpone the general financial collapse for just another few steps ahead, are the flow of funds now being diverted to support needed for the British and U.S. mortgage bubbles. Typical of the onrushing disasters are the continuing efforts of President George Bush to carry out the mission assigned to him by the Federal Reserve System, to loot the U.S. Social Security system, and that gigantic effort to grab future control over all of the world's principal mineral resources which is reflected in such forms as the present petroleum-price

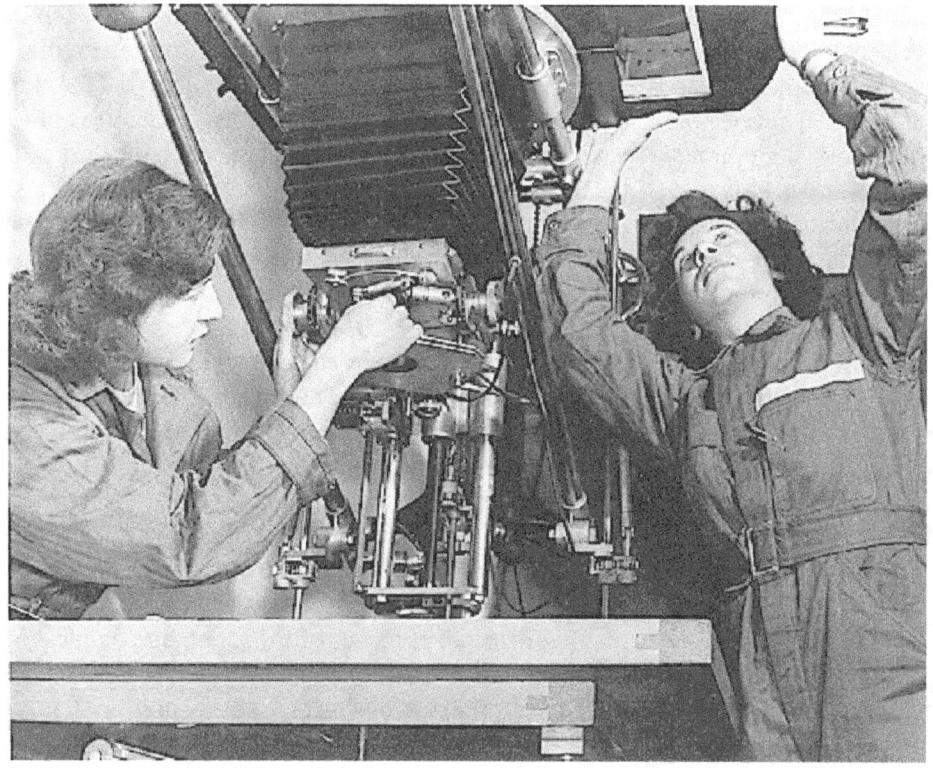

"Lessons learned under President Franklin Roosevelt, from the 1930s recovery-process and the war-time age of the legendary 'Rosie the Riveter,' come into play in relevant modes of policy-shaping" for a national recovery program. Here, women in defense production, 1943.

bubble.

This monetary-financial system is the greatest single obstacle to organizing a recovery from the presently on-rushing financial crash. If that obstacle is not overcome very soon, the world as a whole is already on the brink of a planetary new dark age. Any recovery of the presently collapsing U.S. national economy depends upon immediate, and extensive reforms of that monetary-financial system.

This IMF system is, organically, what is best described in the language of biology as a kind of financial-monetary slime-mold. It is a mass of individual monetary-financial systems which, as in the comparable case of a slime-mold, is composed of individuals, and is yet a single form of existence which controls the fate of all those apparent, participating individualities of which the system as a whole is apparently composed. To understand some of the most essential, controlling features of that system, you must study the image of the life-cyclical behavior of a biological slime-mold, and apply those lessons from the domain of biology to the present form of the IMF system as a whole.

The principal apparent elements of which that mon-

etary slime-mold is composed, are so-called "independent central banking systems," of which the present form of the U.S. Federal Reserve System itself is one rather special sort of variety. In fact, more emphatically in western and central Europe than the U.S.A. itself, these so-called "independent" systems are independent chiefly in the sense that they, as a type of rogue privateer, control governments, rather than the relevant governments controlling them by proper principles of law. In fact, these systems are corporate instruments for common control, by the international system as a whole, a control, by private interests, exerted over national monetary-financial systems. These systems are controlled by syndicates which are composed of a concert of the members of a private club, a private financiers' oligarchy. This is the essential characteristic of the present, floating-exchange-rate form of IMF system.[2]

Therefore, at the same time that a private financiers' oligarchy might be identified with a particular nation, it also functions as an inseparable part of an international entity. This entity, is a kind of financial slime-mold. It presents itself to analysis as in the likeness of a international, planetary slime-mold. Hence, the remarkable similarity of the IMF system as a whole to the metamorphical life-cycle of a global biological slime-mold, the great blob which is currently eating nations and their people.

To understand how to deal with the crisis caused by

---

2. This arrangement may be compared to the form of legalized piracy practiced, as "privateering," under the legal pretext of "letters of marque." In the present case, under a practice in keeping with the same Lockean doctrine of "property" ("shareholder value") used to hold Africans in slavery, the IMF system issues the equivalent of "letters of marque" to private financier syndicates which swoop in, since the 1971-1972 break-up of the Bretton Woods system at the Azores conference, to loot the targetted nation.

the world's present form of monetary-financial system, we must understand that the private aspect of that slime-mold was not originally a product of modern civilization. It is a modern continuation of a feudal species of parasite, a continuation of the very same slime-mold which controlled the European medieval world under the reign of a symbiosis between the financier-oligarchy of Venice and its military ally and instrument, the Norman chivalry. This medieval system was known as the "ultramontane" system, under which national governments of that time, to the extent these were permitted to exist as kingdoms or the like, were under the domination of a greater power, a form of world government, an empire, or as we say today, "globalization." This was the arrangement which was enforced by the use of its chiefly military arm, the Norman Crusaders, the Norman social formation as typified by the House of Anjou or the Habsburg dynasty later.[3]

That medieval system had crashed in what is known to historians as Europe's "Little Dark Age," or "New Dark Age" of the Fourteenth Century. That system collapsed then for internal reasons which are genetically similar to the causes for the presently onrushing collapse of the present, floating-exchange-rate form of world monetary-financial system. The famous case of the Venetian House of Bardi and its thieving picaresque agents, nicknamed "Biche" and "Mouche," were figures comparable to the powerful financier groups and their Enron-like bandits of today.

This crash of the financial system led by the House of Bardi, created the situation in which the forces committed to founding true sovereign nation-states, seized this opportunity to establish modern European civilization, and modern history. This change occurred through a process centered in the mid-Fifteenth-Century, great ecumenical Council of Florence, in which the design of the modern nation-state, such as Louis XI's France and Henry VII's England, temporarily superseded the feudal form of political organization. This occurred as the policy of Cardinal Nicholas of Cusa's **Concordantia Catholica** and **De Docta Ignorantia**, which incorporated, but also superseded the intention of such works of Dante Alighieri as the latter's anti-ultramontane **De Monarchia**. This was the birth of modern European history out of the evils of feudalism.

Unfortunately for us still today, the resurgent power of the same Venetian financier oligarchy which had dominated the medieval world of the Crusades, was able to regain much of its former power through the radiating, disruptive impact of the Ottoman conquest of Constantinople.

The efforts of the Venetian slime-mold system to eradicate the institution of the modern sovereign form of nation-state republic, following the fall of Constantinople, were expressed by the religious warfare which dominated and ruined Europe from the 1492 expulsion of the Jews from Spain until the 1648 Treaty of Westphalia. Since that time, to the present, European civilization as a whole has been dominated by a conflict between two principal forces within European culture as a whole: the sovereign nation-state, as typified by Louis XI's France and Henry VII's England, and also by the Declaration of Independence and Federal Constitution of the U.S.A., versus the modern continuation of the Venetian financier-oligarchy's model of an empire, as the latter is typified today by the global financier hegemony of the Anglo-Dutch Liberal system as typified by the 1763 establishment of an empire-in-fact of the British (e.g., Anglo-Dutch) East India Company.

Since the aftermath of the referenced February 1763 Treaty of Paris, the global history of modern European civilization has been dominated by a persisting controversy between two opposing political systems. On the one side, there has been what is represented by the founding of the U.S.A. as a Federal Constitutional republic. On the other side, we have the revived form of political systems controlled by the financier oligarchy which is, today, an oligarchy which is still an outgrowth of the same slime-mold-modelled Venetian financier-oligarchy.

---

3. During the medieval period, the doctrine of law used to maintain the Venetian-Norman system was the purely fraudulent dogma of "The Donation of Constantine." This was the entirely fraudulent assertion, that the Emperor Constantine had donated the power to rule over the western part of the Roman Empire to the Pope. The Crusades, beginning with the Albigensian Crusade and Norman Conquest of England, were the beginning of that medieval system, which ruled Europe, largely through the conduct of Crusades, until the aftermath of the Fourteenth-Century "Little Dark Age." The actual authority was not the Pope, but the Venetian financier oligarchy and its Norman partners. Under this doctrine only the Emperor could make law, whereas kings and other lesser potentates ruled and made local rules only by the consent of the agency acting in the capacity of the Emperor. The fraud of the "Donation of Constantine" was exposed as a fraud during the proceedings of the Fifteenth-Century great ecumenical Council of Florence. The alternate concept of **Concordantia Catholica** defined the principle of law under which truly sovereign nation-states such as Louis XI's France and Henry VII's England were constituted as the first true nation-states. That Council of Florence was the dividing line between medieval and modern European history.

FIGURE 1

Then and Now: Public Transit, McKeesport, Pennsylvania

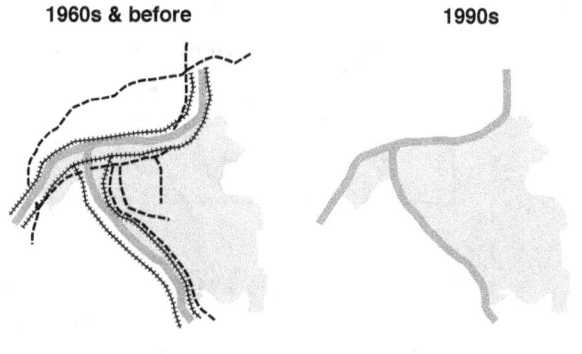

1960s & before   1990s

FIGURE 2

Then and Now: Hospitals in Manhattan, New York, 1960 and 1994

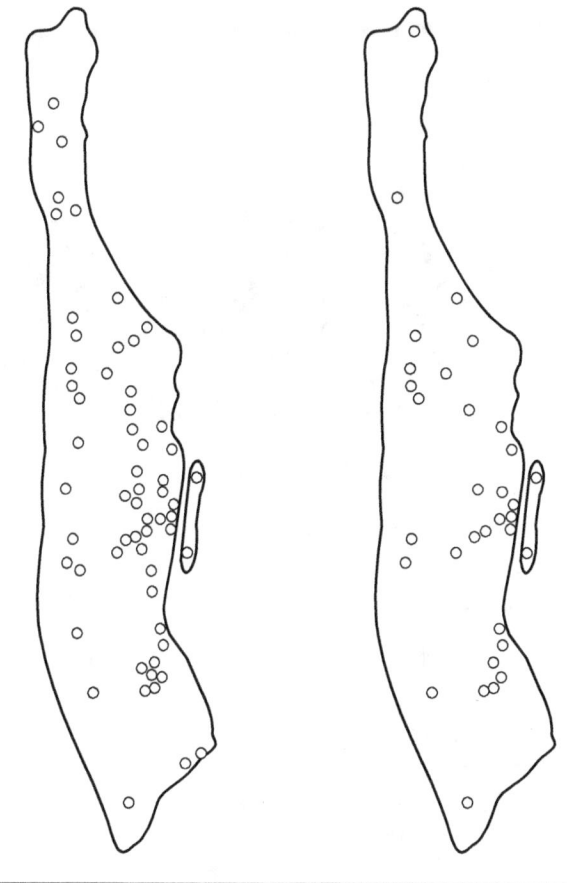

However, the long wave of erosion and decline of Venice's and, later, of its Habsburg client's state power, a decline which continued over the course of the 1648-1848 interval, resulted in the Venetian financier oligarchy's relegation to the ostensibly more limited role within the development of a new form of that same financier slime-mold, the Anglo-Dutch Liberal model of intended world government. The latter form of financier-oligarchical government, emerged as what became the leading power over Europe with what I have already referenced, the February 1763 Treaty of Paris, the treaty which established the British East India Company of Lord Shelburne et al. as a de facto empire.

The combination of the French Revolution, which, contrary to French popular myths, was orchestrated by forces coordinated from Shelburne's London, and the Napoleonic Wars, defined a period of history which ended only with U.S. President Lincoln's victory and the expulsion of the French forces under British Lord Palmerston's Napoleon III from Mexico. The influence of the 1863-1876 consolidation of the intended goal of the U.S.A. as a leading, transcontinental form of sovereign economic power, created a situation of global conflict between the Liberal and American systems.

The 1863-1876 emergence of the U.S.A. as a leading agro-industrial power of the world, provoked the adoption of essential features of the American System of political-economy as the basis for the great, late 1870s economic reforms, modelled upon the successes of the American System, undertaken by Bismarck in Germany, in Japan, in Mendeleyev's Russia, and elsewhere. As in Germany and Japan, these great economic reforms were made in personal coordination with the

man who was Abraham Lincoln's associate, and the greatest economist of that century, Henry C. Carey. This rise in the power of a group of leading nations in Eurasia, as pro-American rivals of the British Empire, prompted the circles around the Prince of Wales, later King Edward VII, to set his nephews, the German Kaiser and Russian Czar, into preparing war against one another, with what the imperial policy of Edward and his Liberal Imperialist Fabian Society thus bequeathed to Europe as World Wars I and II.

Plotting to create such wars on the continent of Eurasia had not been new to the British Empire. It was the Anglo-Dutch Liberals' orchestration of the so-called Seven Years' War against Britain's intended pawn, Frederick the Great's Prussia, which had so weakened the nations of continental Europe that the British East India Company was able to establish virtual imperial

FIGURE 3

U.S. Industrial Belt, Decline in Manufacturing Workers as Percent of Workforce , by County, 1975-2000

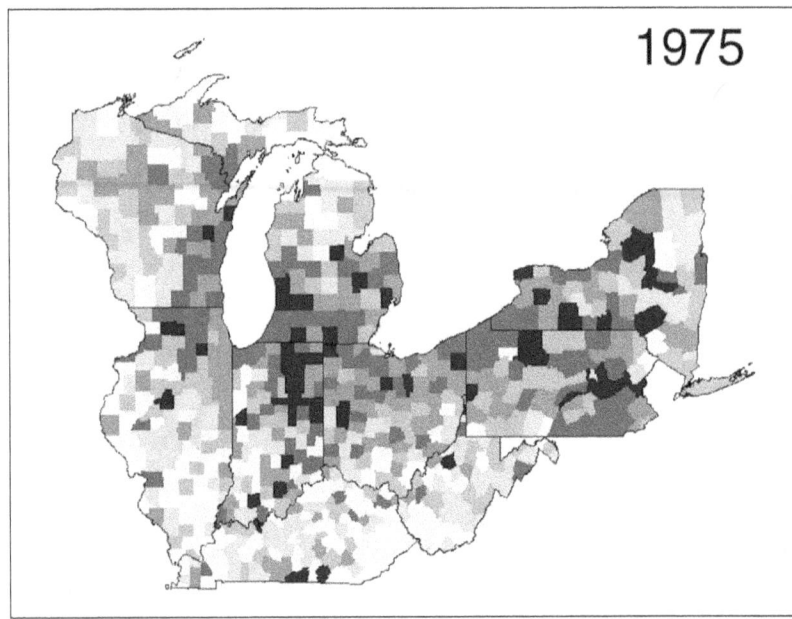

1975

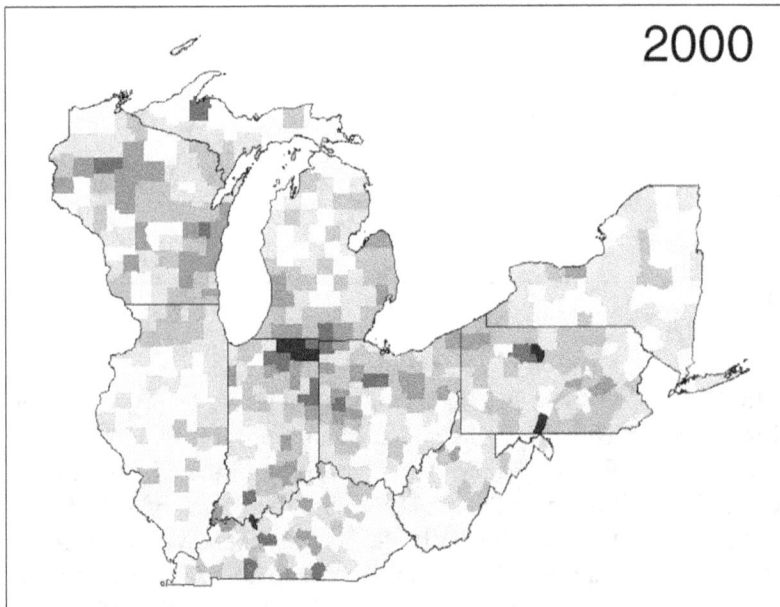

2000

Source: Bureau of Labor Statistics. Map produced by MapInfo.

Darker tones show greater percentages of manufacturing workers.

and central Europe, as the dominant form of national government there still today. That conflict persists to the present day, in the form of virtual warfare, by allied forces of Anglo-Dutch Liberalism from within and outside the U.S.A., against the American System under our Federal Constitution. This, as former Secretary of State Henry A. Kissinger explained to his London audience of May 1982,[4] was the way in which British Liberal circles in Britain used its agents inside the U.S.A., such as the circle around George Pratt Shultz in the Nixon Administration, or Brzezinski as Kissinger's successor later, to orchestrate our national policies and international affairs in such a way as to prompt us to destroy that great economic power we had acquired through the reforms under President Franklin Roosevelt.

Meanwhile, despite the efforts to establish a true Presidential republic on the continent of Europe, as, for example, under President Charles de Gaulle of France, the European parliamentary system is essentially one in which the financier-oligarchical slime-mold continues the pattern of the British Eighteenth-Century model of a political system under

power at the February 1763 Treaty of Paris.

This setting, in the aftermath of the U.S.A.'s power and influence as a great nation, thus defined the strategic setting of conflict for the consequent two World Wars of the Twentieth Century. These have been wars erupting from within what has been established, as the present parliamentary systems of wars-ruined western

the effective control of a philosophically Liberal form of central banking system, a Liberal system which is in

---

4. Henry A. Kissinger, "Reflections on a Partnership: British and American Attitudes to Postwar Foreign Policy, Address in Commemoration of the Bicentenary of the Office of Foreign Secretary," May 10, 1982, Royal Institute of International Affairs (Chatham House), London. The full text is in **EIR**, Jan. 11, 2002.

FIGURE 4
Decline of Annual Raw Steel Output in the Five Top Steel-Producing States, 1973-2003
millions

1973

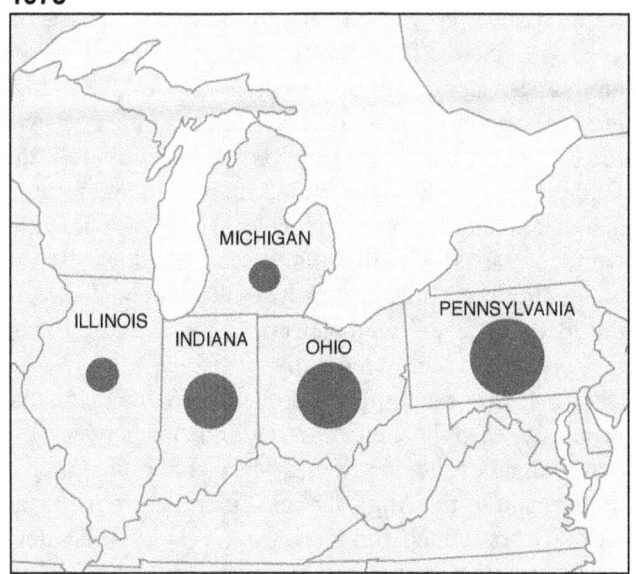

2003

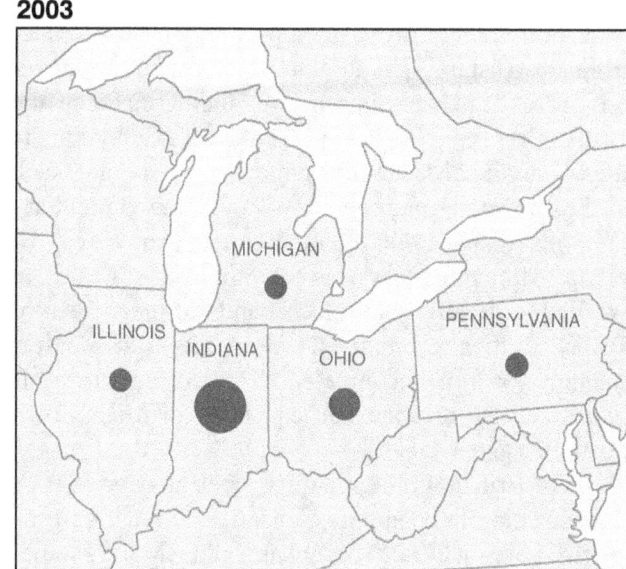

Source: U.S. Geological Survey

These maps show the relative decline in output of raw steel tonnage in Illinois, Indiana, Michigan, Ohio, and Pennsylvania, the top five steel-producing states, shown by the shrinkage of the circles from 1973 to 2003.

fact a creature in the feudal slime-mold tradition.

The struggle to maintain a national banking system in the U.S.A., has been a reflection of the struggle to defend our constitutional system from the overreaching control of the international financier-oligarchical slime-mold which has been far more powerful, globally, than our republic, during most of the past two centuries.

This history summarizes the most essential parts of what it is indispensable to know about the problem which is presented to us by the presently onrushing collapse of the present form of what is essentially a Venetian model of slime-mold system.

Therefore, in times of great crisis, the instinct of all knowledgeable U.S. patriots is to assert the principle of the sovereign nation-state, as expressed by our Declaration of Independence and Federal Constitution: that we must not tolerate any authority in law on this planet higher than the principle of the sovereign nation-state republic. The consequence of that essential principle of our republic, is the principle of national banking, as opposed to the so-called "independent" central banking systems which have, once again, ruled and ruined the world since about the time of the inauguration of our President Richard M. Nixon.

Therefore, throughout all of our national history to date, our combined domestic and foreign policy on matters of economy in general, and trade and finance in particular, such as that expressed by Treasury Secretary Hamilton, has been crafted in recognition that our constitutional system of government, which is based naturally on the principles of national banking, was obliged to operate, most of that time, within the bounds of that alien reality of what had long been the greater combined power of that Venetian-style international financier oligarchy which dominated Europe.

The Lesson From the Soviet Conflict

The experience of the long, nuclear-armed state of post-FDR conflict between our U.S.A. and the Soviet Union contains a lesson which must be learned and applied to the present situation. This pattern of our republic's conflict, as a combined symbiosis and conflict with European Eighteenth- and Nineteenth-Century Liberalism systems, was extended to our relationship with the Soviet Union. The Soviet Union no longer exists, but a brief look at the problem it represented for U.S. foreign policy helps us to define the principled approach in law which must be taken to deal with the slime-mold problem outlined above.

The most essential background to be considered in

studying U.S. relations with the Soviet Union, is the following.

Karl Marx had been absorbed, from his days as a student in Berlin, as a British asset of the Giuseppe Mazzini "Young Europe" complex organized and controlled by Britain's Lord Palmerston. Young Europe recruit Marx, had been subsequently indoctrinated by the British East India Company's Haileybury School in the merely mythical "scientific authority" of wretches such as Physiocrat François Quesnay and the Haileybury School's Adam Smith, Jeremy Bentham, and David Ricardo. Although Marx was something of a genius in working critically within the bounds of the system of British political-economy, the system itself was, unfortunately for him, incompetent. This corruption in his education had relevant consequences for Marx's own economic and social theory.

This British Foreign Office control over Marx's miseducation in economics, under the direction of the British Foreign Office's Urquhart and by Marx's sometime controller Frederick Engels, led to the Marxists' adoption of such pathological doctrines as the "official Marxist" Twentieth-Century myth of Imperialism. The latter doctrine of "orthodox Marxism" attributed the phenomena of imperialism to industrial capital, rather than, as the more intelligent Rosa Luxemburg and our own State Department veteran Herbert Feis have recognized, international loan operations by the Anglo-Dutch Liberal form of the traditional Venetian financier-oligarchy.[5]

The relevant point, bearing on U.S.A.-Soviet diplomacy, of this background on Marx's personal history, is the following.

Under the influence of Britain's Frederick Engels' Thomas Huxley-like doctrine of the "horny hand of labor," the "official Marxist" doctrine became the radically reductionist assumption, that the economic progress of modern industrial nation-states' economic power, was a virtually biological epiphenomenon of the working-class, rather than being an expression of fundamental scientific progress generated through a relevant form of an "intelligentsia" expressing those natural creative powers for scientific and Classical-cultural forms of discovery of universal principle which distinguish *all* persons from lower forms of life such as the great apes. This result of populist and Marxist ideologies congruent with Frederick Engels' influence over Karl Marx, became what proved to be ultimately the fatal flaw of a Soviet Union, in which the frontier achievements of Soviet science's military applications were contrasted with that lugubrious, ideology-driven, bureaucratic dullness which was the crucial factor in the ideologically driven aspects of the collapse of the Soviet civilian sector generally.

Thus, this point of ideological agreement on the principles of philosophical reductionism, between the materialism of the doctrinaire Marxist and the kindred empiricism of the Anglo-Dutch Liberal currents of the world, were reflected in Karl Marx's own foolish deprecation of the Leibnizian American System of political-economy, as in Engels' leading role in prompting Marx's own foolish, uttered deprecations of the American System economists, Hamilton, the Careys, and Friedrich List.

By pragmatic instinct, Lenin, for example, proposed adopting the model of the U.S. economy's achievements as the technological model to be studied and followed by the young Soviet Union. However, the indicated philosophical differences between the U.S. Declaration of Independence and Constitution, on the one side, and both Liberal and Marxist forms of philosophical reductionism, on the opposing side, were always the chief, recurring obstacle to our efforts to establish durably satisfactory relations between the U.S.A. and the Soviet system. The systemic root of this problem in diplomacy, came from the implications of this reductionist element of ideological coincidence between the Marxists and populists, on the one side, and, on the other, the complementary, pro-British, anti-American element of common roots of otherwise diverging Marxist and British Liberal ideologies.[6]

---

5. The degree to which a Karl Marx sponsored by Palmerston's agent Mazzini was duped by Marx's British Library controller Urquhart, is typified by the embarrassing book by Marx himself, in which he accused Palmerston of being a Russian agent! Urquhart was, at relevant times, operating within the "British Museum" as the coordinator ("corresponding secretary") of the far-flung agent-network of Mazzini's "Young Europe" and the "Young America" which later spawned the Confederate States of America. It was the same Mazzini, Palmerston's agent, who created "The First International" at a London meeting, where he personally handed the leadership of the new association over to Karl Marx.

6. The case of the powerful influence of Britain's fiercely anti-American, Cambridge school of systems analysis, as via the Laxenberg, Austria-based International Institute for Applied Systems Analysis, and the related pro-British orientation of the Andropov circles, typify the savagely destructive effects of the influence of British radical-empiricist modes of thought in fostering the self-inflicted aspects of the collapse of the Soviet economy.

National Archives.

President Reagan announces the Strategic Defense Initiative on March 23, 1983. "Had Andropov merely accepted the offer to discuss the proposal directly, world history would have changed for the better, for all parties concerned, and that immediately."

Marxist theology of that reductionist variety was often a crucial factor in the recurring tendency among socialist systems and political currents, toward endemic preference for the British ideology expressed by fervid U.S. hater Bertrand Russell against the legacy of the U.S. Constitutional tradition, and also even the U.S.A. as such. On this point of ideology, the traditionally fascist element among followers, such as Britain's fascist G.K. Chesterton, of Franco's Hispanidad dogma, and Yankee-hating leftists, often converged, or "swapped ideological spit," as the saying goes.

This was a pivotal, if often less widely understood problem for President Franklin Roosevelt, who was not a socialist, but a Yankee in his family's Hamiltonian tradition. Roosevelt, in dealing with the rising industrial trade-union movement during the second half of the 1930s, and later, like his wife, had to consider the factor of socialists in the union and related movements, but was no leftist himself. It has continued as a challenge to U.S. foreign policy to the present time. Our contemporaries' own failure to understand the fallacies underlying this conflict, has often worked against the best interests of our nation, and is a problem which also arises in other disguises in dealing with certain important aspects of our republic's foreign-policy problems and major blunders in several areas, still today, when

the Soviet Union is no more.

The world has entered a phase of its development, as the instance of thermonuclear arsenals merely typifies this, in which the empiricist doctrines of Thomas Hobbes and his like can no longer be tolerated. In today's world situation, the existence of civilization on any part of this planet and the adoption of the principles of the 1648 Treaty of Westphalia become synonymous. Rather than statecraft based on the presumption of peace through negative principles, such as the Bertrand Russell gang's creation of the lunacy of Mutual and Assured (Thermonuclear) Destruction (MAD), there can be no durable form of constructive relations among nations, except on the basis of common positive, rather than merely negative principles.

The most dramatic example of this problem is the case of the foolish Soviet General Secretary Yuri Andropov's reckless rejection of U.S. President Ronald Reagan's public proffer of cooperation in a Strategic Defense Initiative (SDI), an offer which the President had made in a live television address of March 23, 1983. I had been on the inside of the discussion of this with the Soviet government, conducting a back-channel on that President's behalf, and had warned the Soviet government, a month prior to President Reagan's address, that rejection of the President's offer, were he to deliver it, would mean a collapse of the Soviet economy "in about five years." It took six years, rather than my 1983 estimate of approximately five, before the onset of that disintegration of the Comecon which led, rather quickly, into the break-up of the U.S.S.R. itself. Any doubts, still today, of the President's sincerity in making the offer, are simply incompetent, counterproductive babbling.

Had Andropov merely accepted the offer to discuss the proposal directly, world history would have changed for the better, for all parties concerned, and that immediately. President Reagan's object was simply to secure an agreement by which to efficiently rid the world of nuclear-armed missiles. I shared the President's outlook on that entirely; but I also understood, as did leading military and other circles within both the U.S.A. and western Europe with whom I consulted in our common effort on this account, that the possibility of securing his goal in this matter depended on forcing the world to return to the policies of a science-driver economy in such a way as to change the character of the strategic conflict in a crucial way. From my discussions with them during this period, this point was understood by leading military circles of France, in Germany, and in Italy, among others. By making possible the outflanking of missile-borne thermonuclear barrages by an agreed commitment to a "crash program" of qualitatively superior technologies on all sides, we would create a new kind of global balance of power, in which cooperation in scientific-technological progress of economies would be a dominant self-interest of all nations involved.

Had Andropov simply said, "Let us talk about what you have offered," a qualitative shift in the geometry in world politics and strategy would have followed, more or less inevitably. Whatever Andropov's twist of mind in reacting in the reckless manner he did, the lesson of that experience is the role of a lack of ability to grasp the advantage of a positive basis for agreement, an incompetence, a cultural defect with profound moral implications, which was exhibited as clearly by the opponents of the President's proffer even within his own administration, and within the Democratic Party, as by the sheer reckless folly shown by Andropov. On both sides, the opponents of the SDI proffer were acting as barbarians unwilling to test the waters of a civilized solution to the most urgent problem immediately before them,

As President Reagan made his offer, the sharks, in his own administration, in the Democratic Party, and elsewhere, were waiting in hope that Andropov would, in fact, summarily reject the President's offer. This opposition to the President's policy came from those in both U.S. parties who had a vested factional interest in the "post-industrial" doctrines which the 1971-1972 wrecking of the Bretton Woods system had been designed to bring about. A cooperative crash-program dedicated to the dual-use application of the higher order of physical principles expressed in the SDI proposal, would have meant a return to the kinds of international economic policies which the Nixon administration's action of 1971-1972 had been intended to destroy.

So, after we have taken into account the fact that the 1945-1989 conflict between the U.S.A. and U.S.S.R. was artificially induced by the co-thinkers of Winston Churchill, Averell Harriman, Harry Truman, et al., the ability of the war-makers to arrange and maintain that nuclear-weapons conflict over decades, depended upon the lack of a developed philosophical basis for a shared affirmative principle of cooperation on technological cooperation between the U.S.A. and U.S.S.R. This source of difficulty was not unique to the case of U.S.A.-U.S.S.R. relations. So far, the relations among states on this planet, including within the UNO itself, are based, still today, essentially on a notion of balance of deterrence, rather than efficient, as distinct from merely romantically sentimental, notions of the common aims of mankind. So, the Soviet Union is now long past, but the Hobbesian philosophical source of the conflict which had been associated with its existence remains as a curse upon the world at large today.

The basis in demonstrable moral law for dealing with the crucial problem which monetary-financial "slime-mold" represents in the present crisis, lies in a principle which is denied among empiricists and monetarists alike: *the principled difference between man and ape.* I explain.

Put to one side the question, whether the similarities of form between man and ape do, or do not reflect the emergence of human intelligence from an internal development of a group of species associated with the outward form of the higher apes. Notably, the potential relative population-density of a higher ape on this planet during any part of the approximately two millions recent years, represents a potential not in excess of millions, whereas we represent more than six billions today. Man is not a different species of animal, but a qualitatively different order of existence, based on the function of human cognition which is absent in all the beasts. The relevant, scientifically, experimentally crucial functional distinction of man from beast, lies in those cognitive powers of the individual person through which the discovery of experimentally validatable universal physical principles of the universe changes society's practice in ways which increase the potential relative population-density of a specifically human culture.

These relevant discovered principles are of two types, those of physical science and those which we associate with the ancient Greek notion of Classical forms of artistic culture. The first type refers to man's interaction with the world around him; the second type refers to the discovery of principles of social cooperation which are essential to the social realization of the benefits of those discoveries in the form of increase of the society's potential relative population-density.

Even from a bare notion of social benefit, it is the power of the individual human to discover and transmit such discoveries of universal principle, which makes the existence of each person implicitly in the vital interest of society as a whole, in the presently continuing interest in the outcome of earlier, as much as present and future generations. The benefits of scientific progress typify this. The discovery and transmission of such discoveries express what we regard as the cognitive immortality of the mortal human individual.

This notion appears within U.S. constitutional law in two congruent expressions. First, as Leibniz's "the pursuit of happiness," which serves as the crucial positive principle of law, in rejecting the doctrine of John Locke, in the 1776 U.S. Declaration of Independence, and the concept of *agapē*, as from Plato's **Republic** and from such sources as the Christian Apostle Paul's **I Corinthians** 13. The latter is expressed as an integral part of the supreme principle of law presented by the *Preamble* of the Federal Constitution, the superior obligation *to promote the general welfare*. It is also expressed, in other words, as the central principle of law, *the advantage of the other*, in the 1648 Treaty of Westphalia,

To bring those principles effectively into play, we must assure the immortality of the worthy contribution of the individual through the creation of sovereign nation-state republics. By this means, we assure to the individual the immortality of his or her contribution to the welfare of mankind. To that purpose, if we are wise, we endow crafted forms of government with a durable commitment to the principle by means of which the continuity of such wealth of ideas that links the past, present, and future of humanity is affirmed. The power thus embodied in a constitutional form of sovereign nation-state must therefore be embedded in the mission of government, and exert supremacy over all other forms of agreements respecting government.

This arrangement therefore requires that relations within and among states must be based on shared commitment to affirmative principle, rather than a silly, Kantian negation of the merely negative principle of conflict.

The matter of law posed by the Venetian-style slime-mold form of monetary-financial system today, must be addressed from this principled vantage-point.

1.2 The Issue of International Law

Once we affirm the principle of the sovereign nation-state as the highest form of law of government, the financial institutions become merely subjects of the law of and by governments so constituted. In the one case, the required form of government is that of an individual sovereign state. In the second, it is a concert of agreement among individual such sovereign nation-states, or an international monetary system in which an assembly of financial institutions is accountable to the superior authority of a concert of sovereign states. All relevant law and its application is properly subject to the universal principle of the promotion of the general welfare, otherwise known as *the common good*.

These considerations provide us the only tolerable approach under natural law toward solving the crisis represented by the presently onrushing collapse of the world's present monetary-financial system.

Under that notion of law, most of the existing central banking systems are merely private, bankrupt entities, subject to being taken in receivership, for reorganization, by relevant governments. The principle of natural law which applies to such situations, is the obligation of the government to promote the general welfare by whatever means are available to accomplish that result.

Today's IMF is essentially bankrupt in fact. The fact that it is used, together with member governments, as a vehicle for promoting the uttering of fictitious credit, that even in such extreme forms as financial derivatives, enables it, as it is said, "to paper over" its actually perilous financial condition, until now.

The action by Federal Reserve Chairman Alan Greenspan, in the aftermath of the October 1987 New York stock-market crash, to unleash a flood of what have no more intrinsic merit than gambler's side-bets, financial derivatives (e.g., hedge funds), is the most monstrous of the mechanisms by which the hopeless bankruptcy of the IMF is papered over with the delusions of its admirers. The mixing of the nominal proceeds of financial-derivatives transactions with the regular accounts of the financial market, has now unleashed a degree of overall inflation by worthless assets within

FIGURE 5
Decline in U.S. Machine Tool Output, 1974-2003

(Thousands Units Shipped)

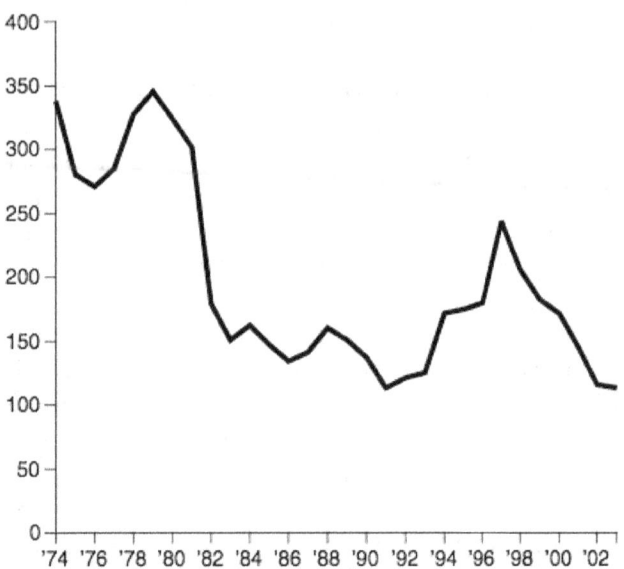

Sources: Association for Manufacturing Technology; U.S. Census Bureau.

the system, such that the potential inflation points either, to straight up, or to a puncturing of the overinflated balloon which leads immediately to a general breakdown crisis of the system as a whole. We are presently bumping up against the self-defined limits, the characteristic internal boundaries, of that IMF system as a whole.

The relevant principle of natural law for such a case, even a far less severe case than the present situation, is that the public interest must be preserved by action of sovereign government to take the bankrupt system into receivership for financial and related reorganization. Now, instead of the IMF slime-mold's putting nations into bankruptcy, the nations, as sovereigns, take the responsible action in the interest of the common good, to take the currently bankrupt IMF system into receivership for reorganization.

The typical victim of today's popularized ideology may follow my argument here up to a certain point; but, then, as if he had experienced a jolt, he blurts out, "But, that is all wrong. You can't do that; that is against everything I have been taught to believe"—*since ancient Babylon*. He (or, she) is a victim of brainwashing in the Liberal system. It is virtually impossible to induce him (or, her) to break with that brainwashing simply by as-

serting the need for a different system than he has been conditioned to believe is self-evidently right. You must change the subject of the discussion, as Alexander Hamilton did, for example, in his famous three reports by the first George Washington Administration to the U.S. Congress. You must say, "Forget money for just a moment. Let us look at how an economy functions in purely physical terms," as Hamilton did in his December 1791 report **On the Subject of Manufactures**, in which he focussed attention on the nature of economic development of a national economy in terms of the interdependent actions of a rural agricultural and urban industrial economy through the medium of development of the basic economic infrastructure by means of which their interaction is integrated.

Monetary systems, and their institutions, must be designed and regulated for the mission of ensuring the long-term, per-capita physical-economic effects which are consistent with the universal moral principle of the promotion of the general welfare.

Some Relevant History of the Matter

In the economic history of the U.S., the role of money issued by a sovereign was first defined in practice by the Massachusetts Bay Colony by the creation of a form of scrip which was allowed to circulate only in a prescribed way, as credit, within the colony's economy. This was highly successful, as the spectacular progress of the development of technology and prosperity ensured within the colony, up to the point that London-based Anglo-Dutch Liberal interests suppressed the colony's rights.

These early and subsequent developments, which led into the crafting of the principles of the American System of political-economy as the cornerstone of our constitutional system of government, were in fact reflections of the recurring periods of influence of the work of the scientist Gottfried Leibniz in shaping what became the characteristic outlook expressed by our constitutional republic's creation. Some remarks on that background material are necessary at this point; it is necessary to clear away certain widely accepted myths which tend to prevent competent insight into the causes of our nation's economic troubles of today.

In all the most prudent practices in our North America since that time, we have tied money issued by the uniquely sovereign authority of governments to a price of monetary gold, as President Franklin Roosevelt induced the use of a gold reserve system, not a

FIGURE 6

U.S. Nuclear Power Plants, and Cancellations Since 1980

- ● Installed Power Plants
- ○ Cancellations

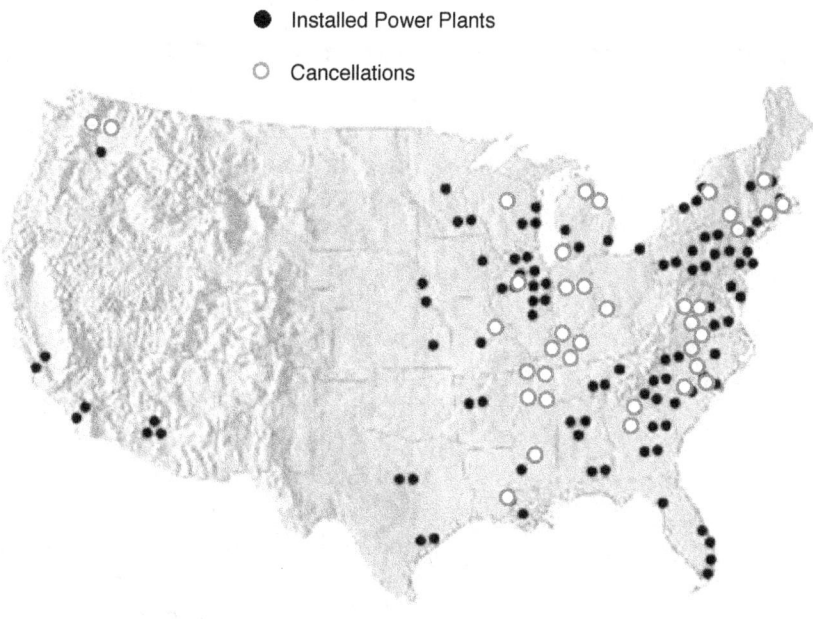

Source: Nuclear Energy Institute

foolish gold standard system, under the Bretton Woods agreements. However, as Hamilton points to the crux of the matter, the maintenance of the value of currency relative to monetary-reserve gold, demands that various forms of regulation must be imposed on the economy by government, to prevent a debasing of the currency. The regulatory measures instituted under President Franklin Roosevelt's administration are typical of the measures required then, and also again today.

Money is an idiot, which knows no lawful principle. It is a necessary, blunt instrument of modern society, but one whose behavior must be controlled by government, to prevent its reckless, brainless impulses from leading our nation into the swamp of ruin which currently popular "free trade" doctrine has put our republic today. Since the founding of our republic, especially after the menacing chaotic situation allowed under the original articles of our confederation, all of the successes of the American System, including even its bare survival under extremely hostile circumstances abroad, have depended upon that set of the principles of regulation of a money economy which separate the American System of political-economy from the Liberal habits which have usually dominated, and often ruined European systems.

The forms of regulation required are those which were destroyed capriciously, by a lunatic campaign of deregulation, under the direction of the Trilateral Commission team lead by Zbigniew Brzezinski during the 1977-1981 Carter Administration. Those actions under Brzezinski et al. then, actions situated within the context of the Nixon Administration's prior wrecking of the Bretton Woods agreements, are chiefly responsible for turning the U.S. economy into the mass of inflation-ridden wreckage it is today.

It was the combination of the floating-exchange-rate monetary system, which occurred through Shultz, Kissinger, et al., under President Nixon, and deregulation of the economy under the direction of Brzezinski's Trilateral Commission's policies, which is chiefly responsible for the wrecking of the U.S. economy over the course of the recent three decades.

Take the need for a progressive income-tax, for example.

The proper regulatory function of a progressive income-tax, is to give income gained in the form of usefully retained earnings in production a qualitatively more favorable consideration than income which is extracted, as money, from production for economically frivolous purposes. This must also recognize that incomes required for reasonable levels of household consumption should be taxed at relatively much lighter rates, if at all. The general intention must be to induce the population to save, by investing in productive improvements in the economy, and also to punish those who corrupt our national currency and credit by diverting large parts of monetary circulation and credit into practices which tend toward the ruin of the nation as a whole over the medium to long term.

Similarly, tariff regulation in matters of interstate commerce, such as airlines, railways, and highway transport, must be shaped to such purposes as promoting the existing and improvement of these functions, and, also, by ensuring that all areas of the nation are able to function in fair competition with others, rather than causing the principal activities of the economy to

FIGURE 7

Decline in Railroad-Track Mileage, 1950, 1970, and 2000 by Region

(Miles of Track)

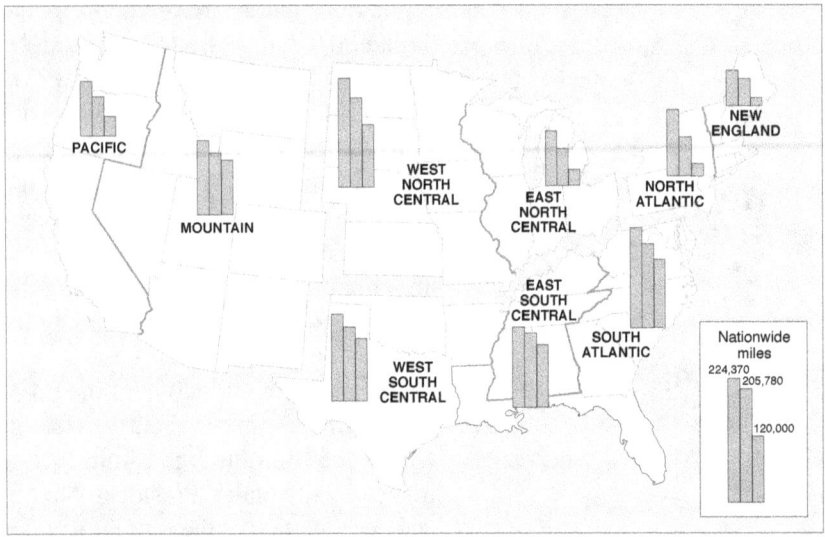

Source: Association of American Railroads.

become congested in a few major markets, while leaving the rest of the nation more or less to rot away by negligence. Look at the way we have destroyed our airlines, our railway system, and so on, under the impact of the orgy of deregulation set into motion during Brzezinski's tenure.

The result of the needed regulatory measures by aid of government action, is the promotion of what has been called formerly a "fair trade" system of pricing. The included purpose of such "fair trade," as opposed to the reckless dogmas of "free trade," is to promote the protection of useful capital investments, and standard of living of households, from the foreseeable effects of allowing the free roving by predatory financial power roaming like pirates under the banner of "the price is right!"

These free trade doctrines which have been used to destroy the U.S. economy, in those and related ways, over a period of slightly more than three decades, have been explicitly copied from the 1776 ranting against the independence of the United States by Lord Shelburne's propagandist Adam Smith. These were the dogmas which Smith adopted by pillaging the intellectual products of his pro-Satanic predecessor Bernard Mandeville, and the writings of the Physiocrats Quesnay and Turgot,

Smith was very clear in his **Wealth of Nations**

attack on the Americans. The pro-Satanic Mandeville of today's Mont Pelerin Society, insisted, as the Society's Milton Friedman has done, that the encouragement of private vice was the source of the public benefit of what is wrongly credited to "free trade" today. The Physiocrats Quesnay and Turgot, from whose writings Lord Shelburne's lackey Adam Smith had pilfered and appropriated most of what he claimed to be fruits of his originality, had based the notion of *laissez-faire* on magical powers presumed to inhere in a titled landlord's status. The use of "the magic of the marketplace" is an apt reflection of the Gnostic, or so-called Faustian principle by which one man is made rich, and the other poor. There is no sane basis for any of the doctrine of "free trade"; the doctrine itself is, like gambling manias, a form of superstition peddled to the credulous.

The development of a competent science of political-economy, was chiefly the work of Gottfried Leibniz over the interval 1671-1716. The outcome of that work was what was known as the science of physical economy. It was this work of Leibniz, as transmitted into the circles of James Logan and the circles of the Winthrops and Mathers of New England, and the circles of Benjamin Franklin, and others, later, which provided the basis for that American System of political-economy whose principle is reflected in the successive craftings of U.S. Declaration of Independence and Federal Constitution.

The essential, physical-scientific basis for the successful circulation of these conceptions as the basis of the American System, had their physical-scientific origins in the Classical tradition of pre-Aristotelean, ancient Greek physical science, as expressed by the concept of *power* (*dynamis*) of Thales, the Pythagoreans, and Plato. This was the same concept central to such work as the founding of modern experimental physical science by Cardinal Nicholas of Cusa, as his **De Docta Ignorantia**. This work was the founding of the modern physical science whose mainstream is represented by the continuity from Cusa, Luca Pacioli, Leonardo da Vinci, and Johannes Kepler, into the work of Leibniz and of such as Gauss and Riemann

Pennsylvania: Counties Meeting Hill-Burton Standard of Hospital Beds per 1000 Persons, 1980 and 2002

Source: Pennsylvania Department of Health.

after Leibniz.

This conception of *power* has taken its modern form since the work of Leibniz, through the work of a student, Carl Gauss, of the same Abraham Kästner, a one-time host of Benjamin Franklin, who had been a key part of the process of delivering to Benjamin Franklin the anti-Locke, Leibniz concept, of "the pursuit of happiness," which served as the keystone of natural law embedded in the 1776 U.S. Declaration of Independence. Gauss's attack on the rabidly empiricist ideologues D'Alembert, Euler, Lagrange, et al., in

Gauss's 1799 doctoral dissertation, was his affirmation of the same concept of *power* central to the work of such as Cusa, Pacioli, Leonardo, Kepler, Leibniz, et al., the concept of *power* employed by the Classical Greek science. This is the concept of *power* (*Kraft*) central to Leibniz's science of physical economy, on which my own original work in economics was based. This is the concept of *power* which was arbitrarily excluded by all of the work in economics in particular, and in science in general, of the empiricists and their modern positivist and existentialist followers.

I summarize the role of the notion of power in the American System of political-economy here, because it has an indispensable role in enabling the economists and statesmen of today to grasp the principles which must be employed to effect a successful recovery of an otherwise now virtually doomed present economy of the U.S.A.

Economy As Physical Science

The key to a science of physical economy is what may be recognized from Aeschylus's **Prometheus Bound** as the Promethean principle, the same principle we encounter in the **Book of Genesis's** definition of man and woman as made equally in the image of the Creator, and assigned to duties consistent with those *powers* (e.g., *dynamis*) with which mankind is uniquely endowed. By means of the unique capacity of the human individual to discover those efficient, universal physical principles which are beyond direct perception by the senses, such as Kepler's unique discovery of a principle of univer-

FIGURE 9
Depopulation, Deindustrialization, Poverty in 10 Michigan Cities

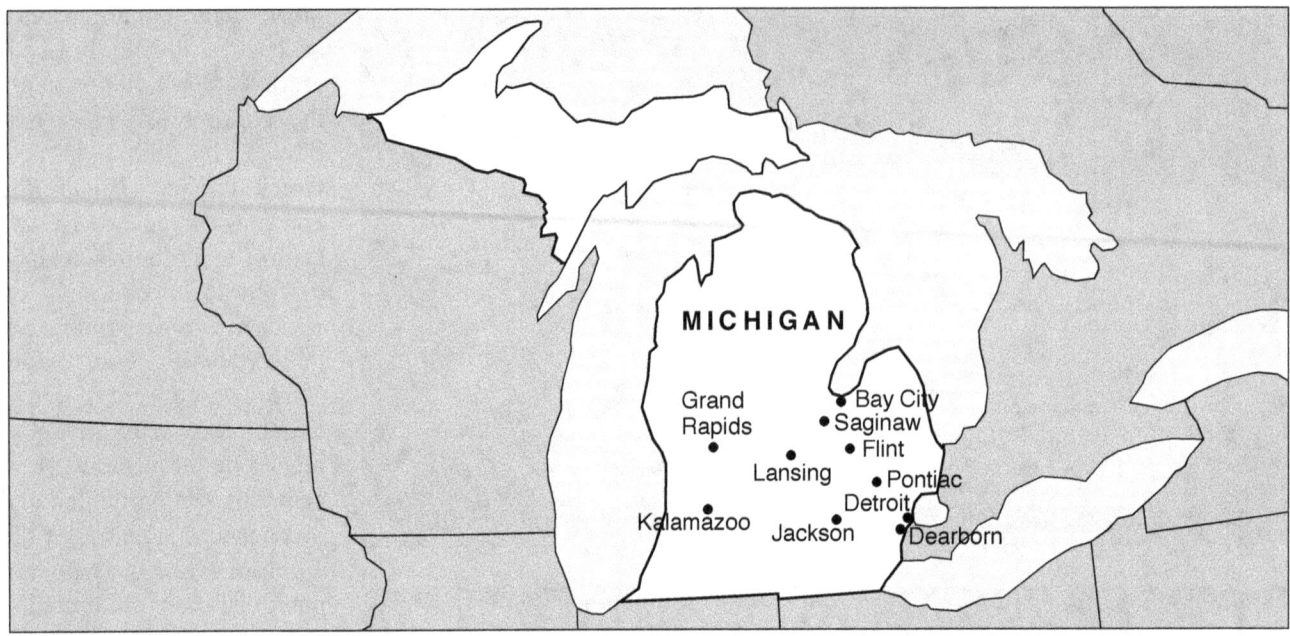

Source: *EIR.*

FIGURE 10
10 Leading Michigan Cities: Population Falls by 29%

(Millions)

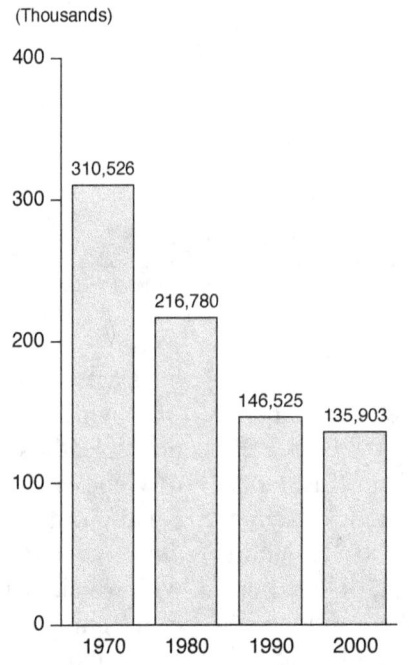

Source: Dept. of Housing and Urban Development, *EIR.*

FIGURE 11
10 Michigan Cities: Manufacturing Workforce Falls by 56%

(Thousands)

Source: Dept. of Housing and Urban Development, *EIR.*

FIGURE 12
10 Michigan Cities: Poverty Rate

(Percent)

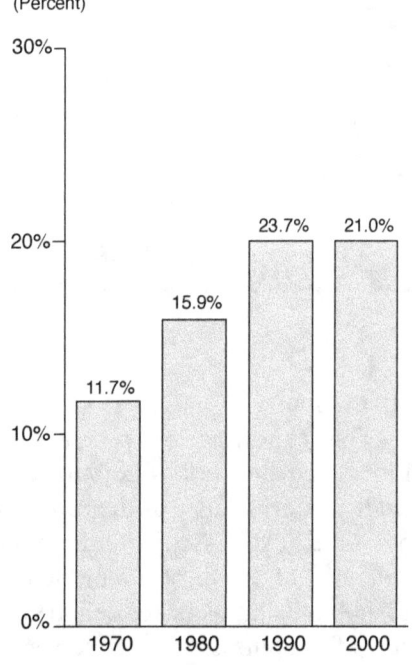

Source: Dept. of Housing and Urban Development, *EIR.*

sal gravitation, mankind is enabled to increase both the number and quality of existence of the typical human individual, an increase implicitly measurable per capita and per square kilometer of the Earth's surface.

It is this conception of power, as recognized by the Pythagoreans and Plato, which is the basis for a science of physical economy: the increase of the productive powers of labor, per capita and per square kilometer.

Here we meet the crucial point of difference between a mere mathematics and a physics, the difference between the relatively passive mere Astronomy of Copernicus and the active Astrophysics of Kepler. It is the difference between observing the motion which has occurred, and conceptualizing the principle—the efficient power—which generates that motion. *In the first, passive discipline of mere mathematics, such as that of D'Alembert, Euler, Lagrange, Cauchy, et al., the effort is made to discover rules by which observed motion will be repeated. In science, such as that of the Pythagoreans, Plato, Kepler, and Leibniz, as distinct from mere mathematics, the objective is to discover the efficient power by which to produce a manifest effect which has never appeared to us in the universe before that time.* That distinction between mere mathematics and physical science defines the notion of *power* in the sense of *dynamis*, or Leibniz's use of *Kraft* in his science of physical economy.

That is the issue of physics (e.g., anti-Euclidean geometry) posed by Gauss's attack on the errors of principle by D'Alembert, Euler, and Lagrange. That is the significance of Riemann's habilitation dissertation, his treatment of Abelian functions, and his emphasis on the conception of Dirichlet's Principle.

In the science of physical economy, our primary focus is on two forms of physical action, beyond the ken of a bald mathematics. The first, is universal physical principles through whose employment mankind's power in and over nature is increased per individual. The second, is those principles of Classical artistic composition whose relevant application is the organization of that social cooperation in use of physical principles which is necessary to translate the application of physical principles into the cooperative social effect we might recognize as social-economic progress in the improvement of the human condition. Both are universal physical principles in type, and belong, ontologically, to what Gauss, Riemann, et al., define for mathematical physics as the complex domain.

It is the transmission of these principles of the class signified by *powers,* which is the means by which increase in man's power over nature, per capita and per square kilometer, is accomplished, as through production.

The principal forms of expression of physical-economic progress in society are agriculture, industry, and infrastructure. The characteristic feature of progress is those forms of technological progress which revolutionize the activity of society in ways which translate the application of power to the increase of the productive powers of labor per capita and per square kilometer. Infrastructure either creates the precondition for such progress in production and consumption, or enhances the expression of the applied productive powers of labor in some necessary way.

In first approximation, physical-economic progress is the result of the injection of principled expressions of scientific-technological progress into the point of production or infrastructure. Actually, the way in which this application must occur to be efficient in modern society, is the ordering of the way in which principled elements of scientific-technological progress are injected into the successive stages of ordering an extended production process, which might be represented by a process-sheet representing stages of production over a significant lapse of time, such as years.

The relevant point of view for understanding this process-view of technological progress in production is best typified by the standpoint of the connection between the work of the experimental scientists and the tool-makers, the starting-point of the process of injecting technological progress into the process represented by the process-sheet cycle as a whole. Looking at the matter from that vantage-point, we are compelled to recognize that it is the injection of technological progress along the pathways depicted by such process-sheets, which is the necessary standpoint from which to study and manage the benefits of technological progress along the pathway mapped by the process-sheet. Scientific-technological progress is, thus, the primary expression of the action on which the success of a modern economy depends.

This shows the way in which the process of education and circumstances of family and other aspects of social life must be ordered to make possible the desired rates of technological progress in society. The economist must therefore avoid the relative intellectual sterility of the mere accountant or mathematician, and adopt the active standpoint of the physicist-toolmaker's view of the successive stages of injection of technological progress, at a certain rate, along the pathways which corresponds to the process-sheet. The role of the household standard of living is defined in terms of the rate of intellectual progress this production-cycle implies.

The determination of estimable "fair price" levels within an economy follows from the study of medium-term and long-term cycles of investment in physical capital in those terms of reference. The money-price of the standard of living of a household, as reflected in the standard of living of a community, serves then to define the unit of reference through which the physical standard of living is correlated with a price-determination of that "basket of physical consumption." Clear thinking on that subject serves as the needed point of conceptual reference for thinking about the relationship between money values and actual physical values.

2. Financing a General Recovery

Organizing a financial recovery from the present state of virtual bankruptcy of the world's present monetary-financial system, has two overlapping phases. There are certain limited, stop-gap measures of a type which must be taken, even within the bounds of the present monetary-financial system, as distinct from the broader actions which require putting the existing system into general receivership for reorganization in bankruptcy.

Take the short-term case immediately at hand, the onrushing collapse of a group of entities fairly described as a "General Motors Complex." We must not be so negligent as to allow that precious productive capacity to be disassembled. Therefore, we must create a "cover" under which the complex is taken into receivership by an entity created by the Federal government, to ensure that essential productive facilities and their employees are held together as a productive capacity.

In this example, the intent will be to create certain new projects, such as in the domain of essential infrastructure requirements of the nation, which will absorb those parts of productive operating potential not presently required for current product-lines of the combined facility taken into tow in this way. A suggested alterna-tive for this purpose would be to create a national program for shifting current passenger and freight requirements from highway to rail, or rail-like modes. I choose this example because it is a likely prospect for very early action, which incorporates several leading features of a large category of options for bringing current national product output, in piecemeal fashion, up to the level of breakeven of the national economy on current account.

The most attractive feature of that option is that it applies essential, leading high-technology potential at the front-end of a growth-driver program, an application which utilizes the employment of a nationally essential, highly skilled, toolmaking segment of the labor-force for a program which generates employment opportunities for a larger population of skilled, semi-skilled, and unskilled labor in the same areas in which the highly skilled occupations are located. It is the kind of program which transmits advanced technologies from the front-end of a program of production, down the chain of subsequent elements in the process-sheet which reaches the intended end-product. This permits the introduction of enhanced technologies at subsequent points in the chain down-line.

It is also an option which has beneficial multiplier effects on suppliers and others whose economic activities intersect the principal axis of the program's sequence. It is the intended acceleration of upgraded technologies along the chain, which provides the anticipatable high-gain in rate of economic return needed to make the project a premium choice of national mission-project.

The object of selecting a key project such as the type needed to prevent a General Motors crisis from becoming a national economic disaster overall, is to set a pattern which can be used as a guide for crafting other project-programs which will tend to become relatively most beneficial.

Parallel to this option for the GM case, we have numerous cases in which urgent action is needed on already specified infrastructure projects, such as those for the U.S. Corps of Engineers.

One of the urgent motives for launching such projects, the urgency of the GM-complex case put aside, is the need to create economic credibility for the idea of an economic-recovery program. Call it the get-out-of-bed principle; if Johnny is getting out of bed on time in the morning, we might tend to believe that he is more likely to arrive at work that day. We as a people, as a government, must convince ourselves and others that we mean business about actually having a general economic recovery, rather than sitting about wailing over the fact that we seem unable to do anything to stop the current hemorrhaging under the Bush Administration. The recovery will require very large masses of long-term credit, much in the quarter-century and longer category; if we can not convince ourselves that we are committed to see that work through to a successful outcome, our ability to mobilize the credit needed will tend to fall toward zero. Getting started on the journey is the first, essential, political-psychological step toward

Education Specialty: Post-Industrialism

During the last 50 years, more and more Americans have been getting undergraduate, graduate, and post-graduate degrees—but in what? Even as our population grew, the percentage of people in their twenties with college degrees has more than tripled, from 7% in 1950 to something more than 22% today. In simple totals, we have, today, about one and a half times as many doctorate and bachelor degrees conferred each year than we did in 1970. The number of masters degrees conferred each year has just about doubled since then. But, what areas of study have kept pace with these increases? And, thereby, which areas of the U.S. productive economic capacities have continued to be renewed and replenished; and which have, on a relative basis, been diminished or degraded for lack of new graduates?

The greatest relative drop in doctoral degrees conferred since the 1920s has been, far and away, in the physical sciences. In the 1920s, '30s, and '40s, fully one-fifth to one-quarter of all doctorates conferred were in the physical sciences. By the late 1970s, only 10% were; and today, fewer than 9%. The simple numbers of master's and bachelor's degrees conferred annually in the physical sciences, from the 1970s to today, have dropped by 50-60%.

In agriculture and natural resources, doctorates conferred annually, as a percentage of the total doctorates, are now below the levels of the 1920s and '30s, having peaked in the '50s and '60s.

Engineering doctorates, overall, have increased from 1% of the total doctorates conferred annually in the early 1920s to 12% in the mid-1960s. A drop to below 8% by 1980 recovered by the 1990s and 2000 back up to mid-1960s levels. However, only half of

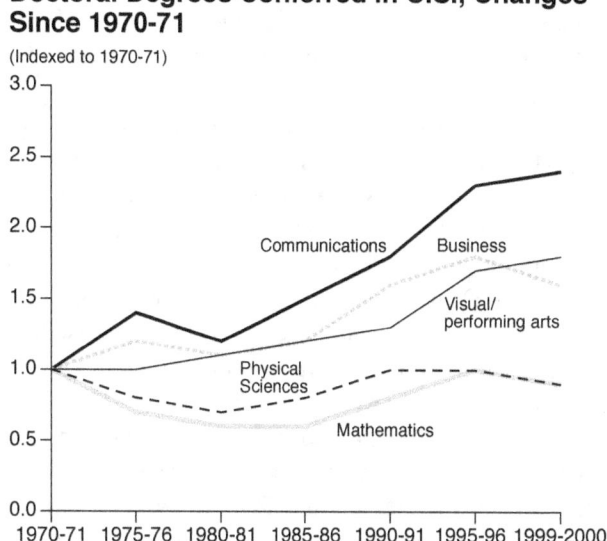

FIGURE 1

Doctoral Degrees Conferred in U.S., Changes Since 1970-71

(Indexed to 1970-71)

Source: EIR

these are U.S. citizens and can be expected to remain in the country. Also, increasingly, engineers are being trained in business practice or in IT, rather than in areas of the physical economy.

So, what about the services and the IT sectors? These areas have either kept pace with, or far exceeded, the overall increases seen in degrees conferred. The number of business degrees conferred annually, including bachelor's, master's, and doctoral, were 2.5 times greater in 2000 than they were in 1970. Not surprisingly, the number of computer and information sciences degrees conferred in 2000 was close to 12.5 times the number in 1970. And, the armies of college graduates in the fields of parks, recreation, leisure, and fitness studies have swelled in ranks by 12 times their 1970 levels.

These figures come from the U.S. Department of Education and the National Center for Education Statistics.

—Judy DeMarco

reaching our destination.

Some things, like that, can be, and must be started immediately, even under the present international-financial monetary conditions. However, proceeding with these preliminary actions depends upon our confidence in our commitment to go all the way with a general reform of the national and international system. We must move now, to convince ourselves that we intend to succeed in the long run; but, to engender confidence in immediate actions of that sort, we must have confidence that we have a workable long-term plan for the journey toward our destination a generation or more ahead.

The ability to generate and sustain the masses of long-term credit needed for a general reorganization and recovery of the world's monetary order, depends upon our willingness to accept nothing less than the replacement of the intrinsically bankrupt, present, floating-exchange-rate monetary system, by a fixed-exchange-rate system congruent with the essential features of the original Bretton Woods system. The essential differences between then and now are four.

First, the U.S.A. is no longer capable of carrying the new fixed-exchange-rate system as the U.S. dollar was used to back up the original Bretton Woods system. There must be a consort of principal guarantors of the new system.

Second, the growth of the world's population, and other qualitative changes, such as a new perspective on the challenge of providing raw materials, present us with problems which did not exist in that form and degree a half-century ago. Today, especially with the currently rabid speculation on future control of the planet's essential raw-materials assets, new measures of regulation to end such speculation are needed as a precondition for a stable new world monetary order.

Third, the pivotal feature of a successful new world monetary system, will be the emerging relationship between western and central Europe, on the one side, and the Eurasia group centered upon the triangular cooperation among Russia, China, and India. This prospect in Eurasia as a whole is now the pivot on which the rational organization of the set of relations within the world economy now depends. As a side-effect of this, the composition of world trade will tend to shift from emphasis on final products, to trade in intermediate products among nations.

Fourth, the conduct of trade among nations will be based upon a span of two generations in principal long-term trade-agreements among nations. The need for increasing capital-intensity in developing assured supplies of greatly increased requirements of raw materials, will be among the leading determining considerations in defining a fifty-year cycle as the basis for long-term trade agreements. There will be a similar effect generated by the increased ration of long-term capital investment in high-speed, land-based modes of transportation of passengers and freight across not only vast continental spans, but, as the implications of a Bering Straits link of Asia and North America implies, intercontinental spans.

The New Role of the U.S. Dollar

Now, look at the indispensable future role of the U.S. dollar in the context of what I have written here up to this point.

The present world monetary-financial system is based on denomination of the U.S. dollar as a reserve currency. Any precipitous collapse of the value of that dollar, whether spontaneous or negotiated, would create a situation under which a chain-reaction collapse of the entire planet into a new dark age, comparable to that of Europe's mid-Fourteenth-Century "Little Dark Age," would ensue immediately. The possibility of a transition from the present planetary situation of imminent general collapse of the entire system depends upon fixing the value of the U.S. dollar at approximately its current valuation, and a comparable fixing of the standard for gold reserves under a fixed-exchange-rate system. There exists no sane alternative to these measures at this time.

For example, when we take into account the vast amount of U.S. dollar holdings currently outstanding in nations such as China, Japan, Korea, and elsewhere, any presently virtually inevitable, early chain-reaction collapse of the dollar's valuation, if permitted to proceed, would, in itself, create an impossible situation for all parts of the planet today.

The only way in which a "new dark age" variety of global collapse could be averted, is to create a new, fixed-exchange-rate, gold reserve, world monetary system which is built around the starting-point of fixing the price of virtually all leading currencies at approximately their price at the current instant. This requires, essentially, immediate action which converts short- to medium-term *legally and morally legitimate* claims, *as if automatically*, against the dollar, into long-term claims against the dollar held as a reserve currency within a gold-reserve-based, fixed-exchange-rate system comparable to the original fixed-exchange-rate system launched by 1944-1945 agreements.

U.S. economic, financial, and monetary policy must *therefore* be changed now to conform to the requirements of supporting that general monetary agreement. Any sane government of the U.S. would agree to this readily, recognizing that this is the only available means for preventing a collapse of the world economy, including the U.S.A. itself, into a deep, deep pit of despair.

This must be accompanied and expressed by physical-economic-policy reforms within the U.S.A. and among nations, which conform to meeting the obligations implicit in that altered role for the U.S. dollar as a global reserve currency. This also means a general revision of trade and tariff agreements among nations in ways needed to support the replacement of the presently, so-called "globalized," "free trade" order by a "fair trade"-based order. This change will be supported by nations which wish to survive, simply because their survival depends upon the adoption and faithful implementation of such new agreements.

The quality of these reforms as constituting a long-term valuation of the world's reserve-currency-based system, depends upon crafting arrays of trade and related treaty agreements among principal nations of the world on the basis of quarter- to half-century commitments to building a global economic basis in long-term physical-capital formation in basic economic infrastructure, and upon the novel, but presently indispensable included feature of a global raw-materials development, supply-and-pricing policy.

The pattern for such complementary monetary-financial and economic reforms is emerging from growing long-term cooperation between the principal industrialized nations of western and central Europe with the long-term Eurasian development perspectives implicit in growing relations between such nations of western Europe with the programs emerging around the Russia-India-China Triangle. The same principles must be extended to Africa, especially sub-Saharan Africa, and to the coordinated development within the Americas, and also elsewhere. It is the accumulation of long-term development agreements of such forms which provides the foundation for securing the stable long-term valuations needed within the newly reformed system as a whole.

Without these emergency actions to change the world system now, a prolonged planetary new dark age were the inevitable outcome of the adoption of any contrary opinion.

Endnote

However, critical sticklers for the details behind General Johnson's design for National Recovery Act ("The Blue Eagle," or NRA) should note the following. The underlying principles of Franklin Roosevelt's approach to the challenge of the 1930-1945 interval remained the same commitment to the Hamiltonian tradition which he reflected in a paper written in the context of his Harvard graduation, and during the later studies of the American System, which occurred during his struggle to overcome the impact of poliomyelitis. However, although that President's policies were an explicit alternative to, and opposition to the Nazi regime under Hjalmar Schacht's Hitler, at that time the Coolidge and Hoover administrations, and much U.S. popular opinion, had been pro-fascist. So, his first campaign for the Presidency and the NRA days expressed influences of the fascist ideology of both Republicans and American liberals, such as John Dewey, et al., of that time. For example, the leadership of the Democratic Party at that time, which was openly, even savagely anti-Franklin Roosevelt, was essentially pro-fascist, like the so-called neo-cons and similar "conservatives" today. So, the ideology of the late 1920s, under Presidents Coolidge and Hoover, contained a lot of faddish leaning toward the impression of Mussolini's regime at that time. It was with FDR's alliance with John L. Lewis's campaign for industrial democracy, which provided the social-political basis for FDR's ability to wean the U.S.A. majority opinion from the relics of fascist sentiment. So, the viable currents in the Democratic Party of today, are tending to break with the strong anti-FDR influence expressed by the Congress for Cultural Freedom's destructive influence in creating the "cultural paradigm shift" exhibited among the generation of university age during the late 1960s and 1970s. With President FDR, it was the "Hamiltonian" legacy of which came to the fore in the evolution of the Presidency during that period. This was not a change in FDR's personal outlook; it was a change in the currents of public opinion with which any President of the U.S.A. is compelled to deal politically. For purposes of comparison, you might consider the different kind of example from my own case; to understand me today, you must look into the crucially formative, virtually "genetic," pre-1949 phases of my own original discoveries in the Leibnizian science of physical economy. In the case of every significant figure in history, there are deep structures which persist, and also relatively superficial phases which reflect a period of adaptation to the cultural setting in which that figure found himself or herself. In my adult lifetime, I, too, have had to ally with constituencies whose axiomatic opinions I did not fully share, as in certain alliances I adopted in good faith in my repeated role in opposing pro-fascist currents in our own nation, such as those pro-fascist currents associated with the Truman Administration and with the Nixon Administration and its current since.